Vintage Botany Botanical Flower Prints (Floral Ephemera Series 1)
By C. Anders

This book is a work of non-fiction. Images in this book may have been retouched. No part of this book maybe be reproduced, scanned, or printed in any printed or electronic form without permission from the author. Please do not participate or encourage piracy of copyrighted materials in violation of the author's rights.
Purchase only authorized editions.
Copyright © 2018 by C Anders. All rights reserved.

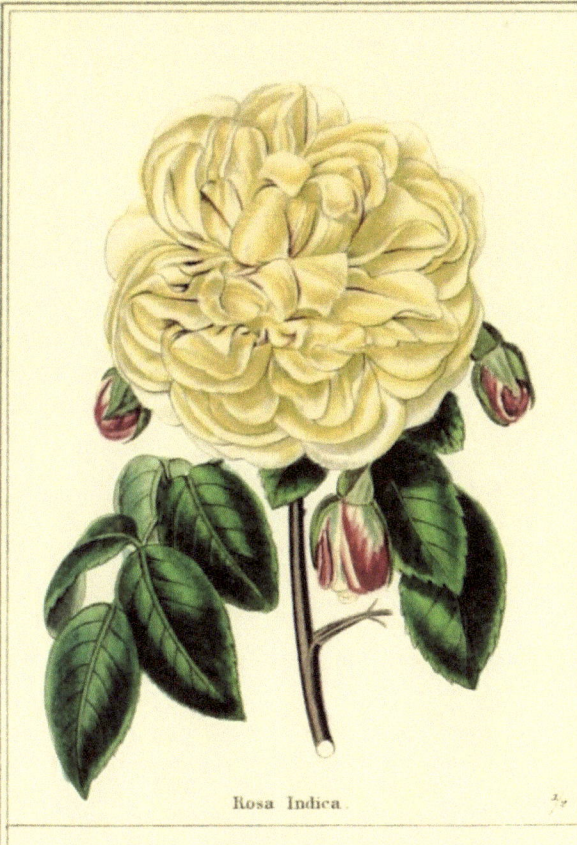
Rosa Indica.

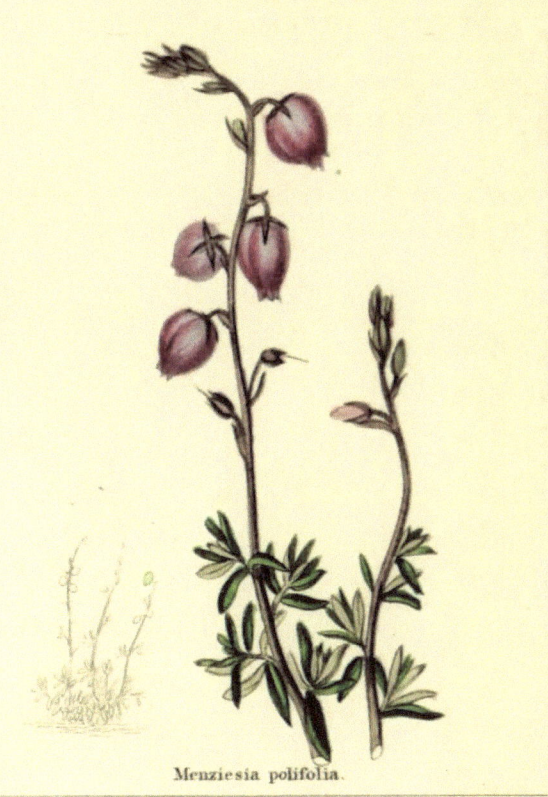
Menziesia polifolia.

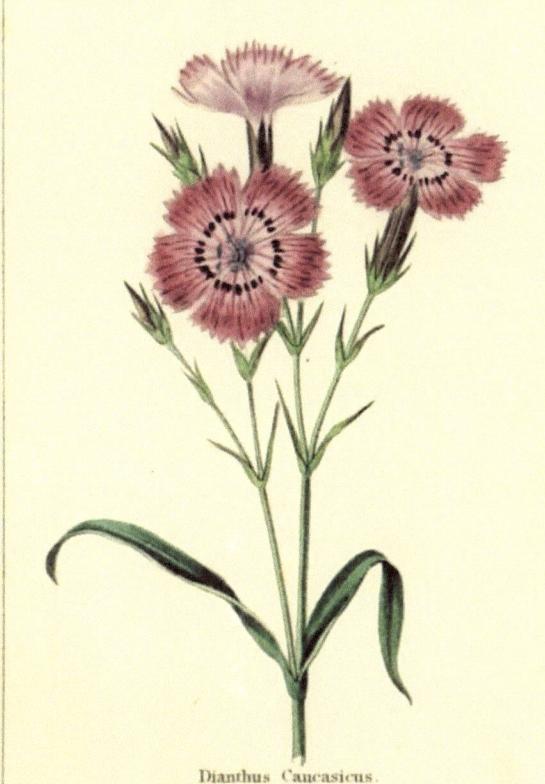
Dianthus Caucasicus.

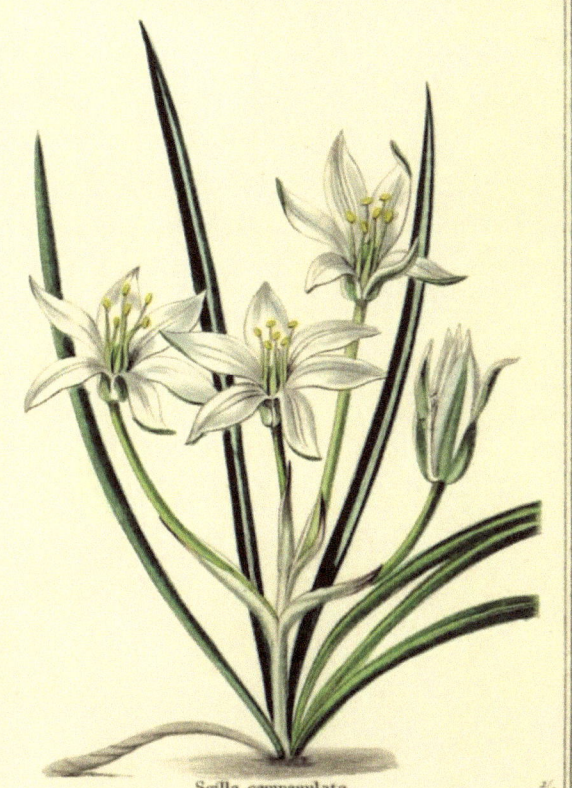
Scilla campanulata.

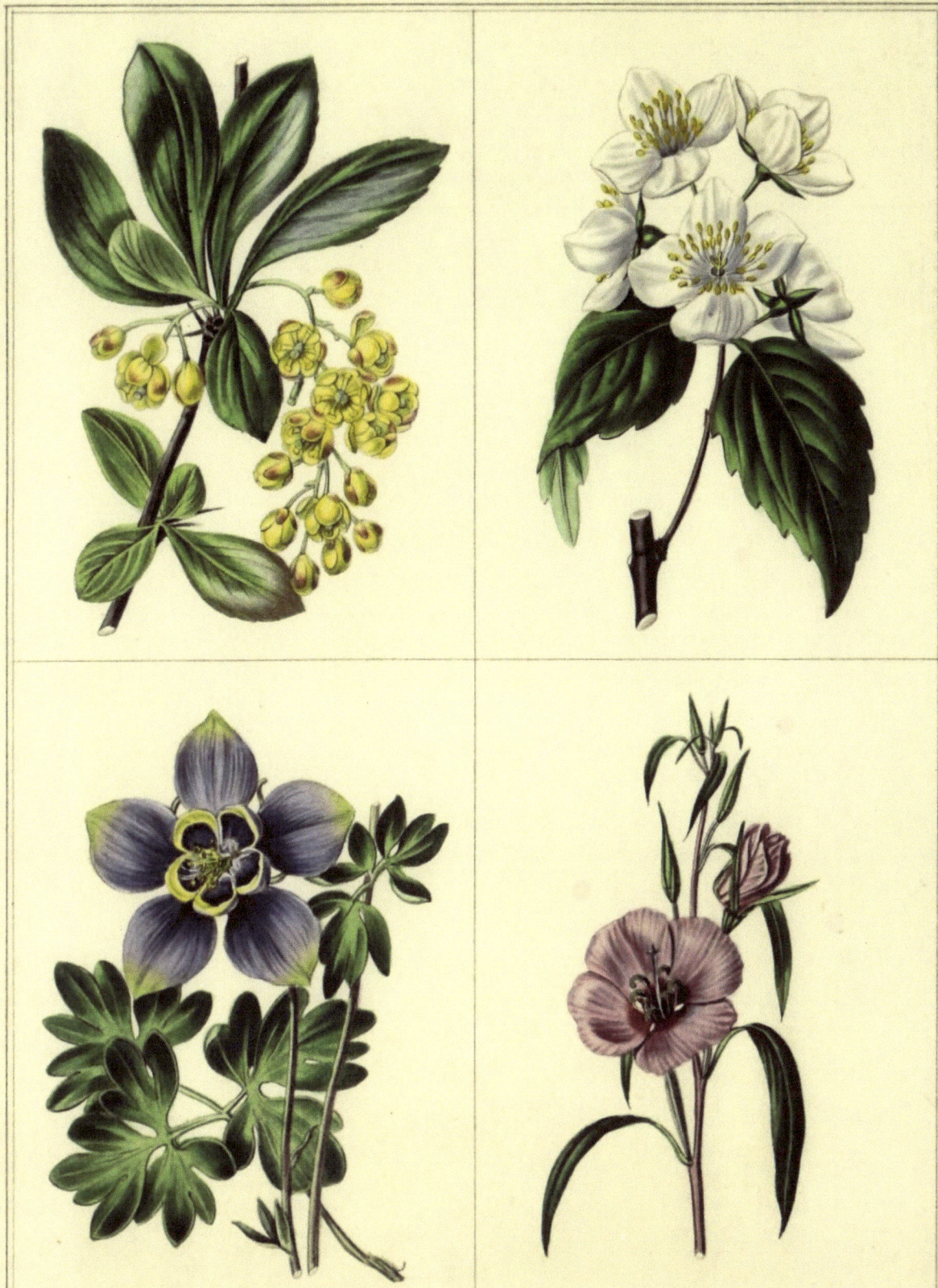

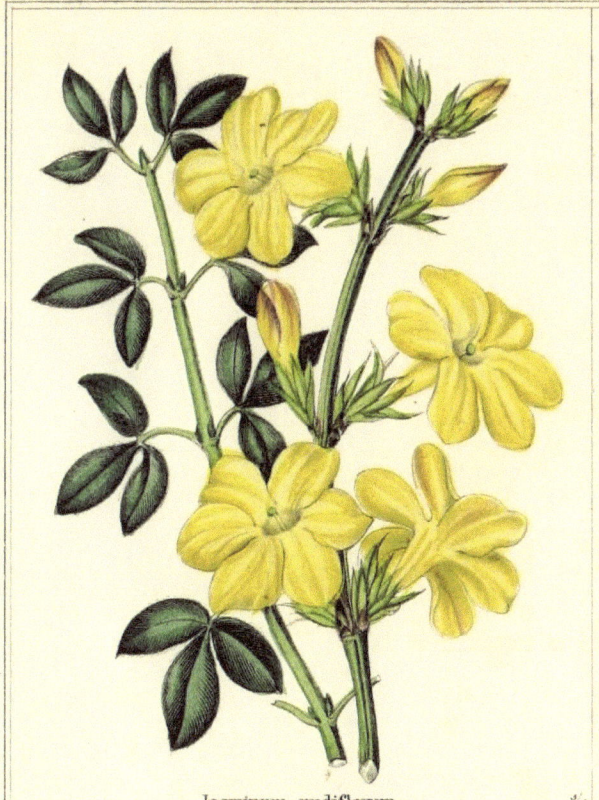
Jasminum nudiflorum.

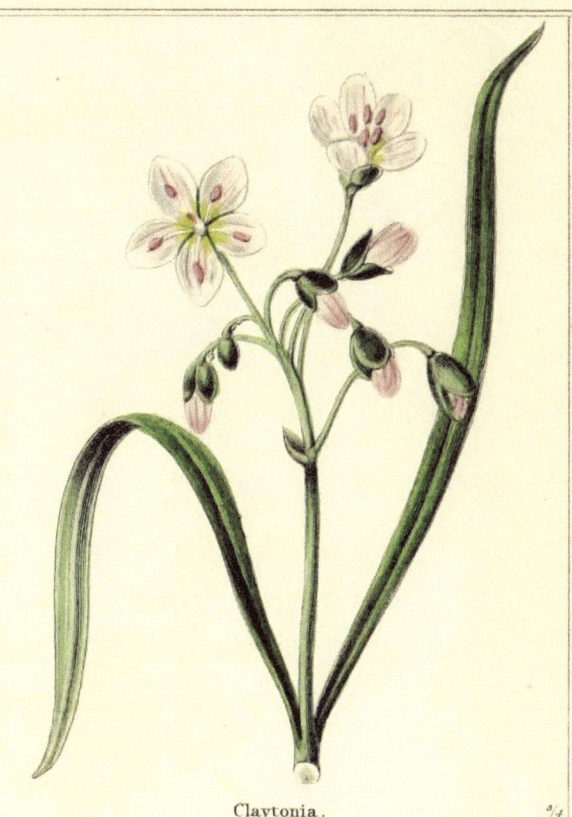
Claytonia.

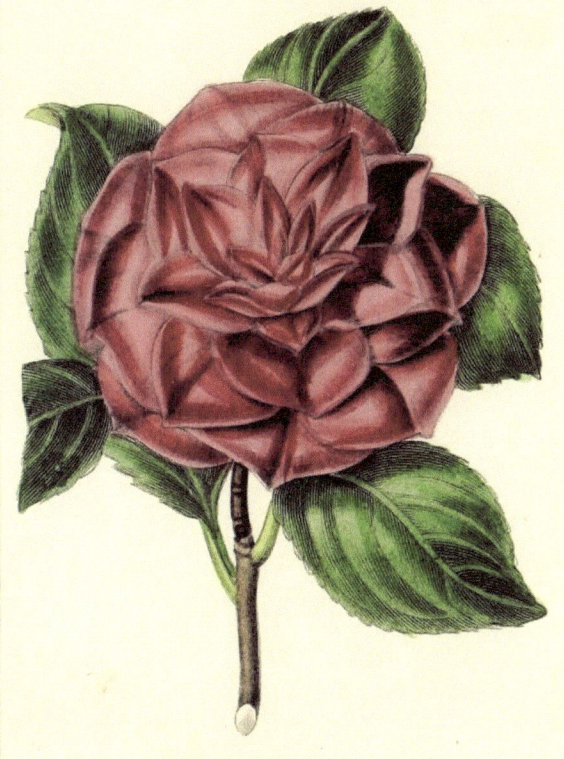
Camellia Japonica.

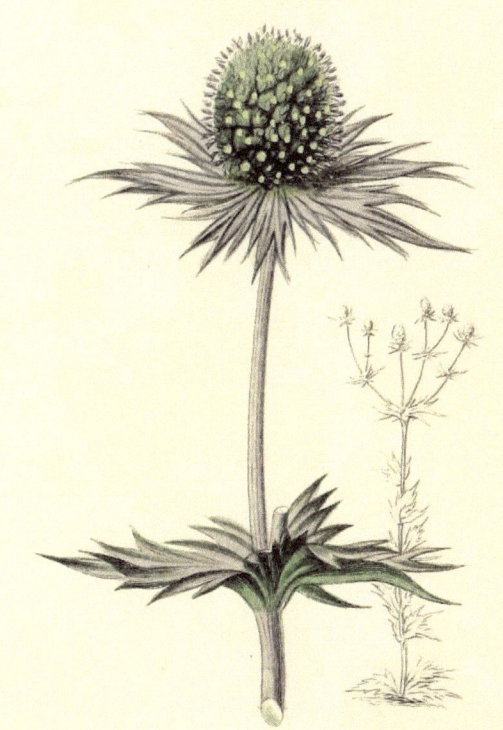
Eryngium giganteum.

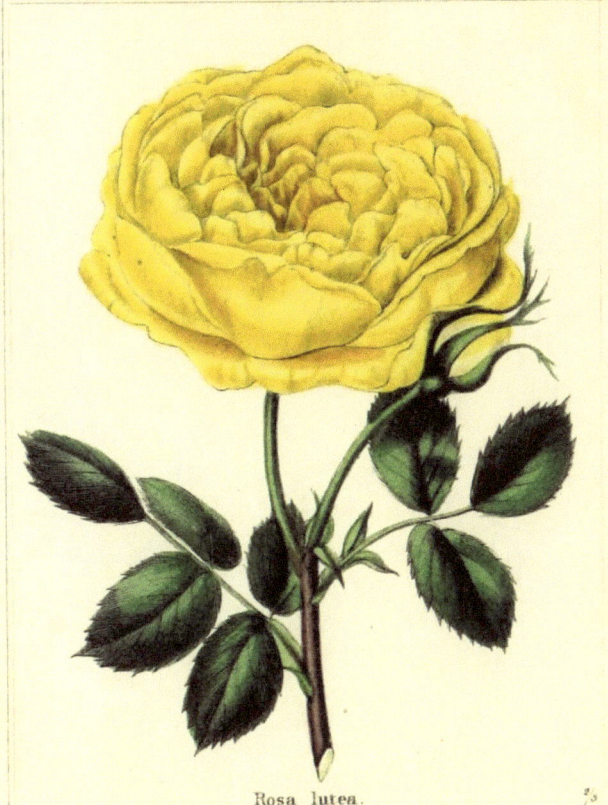
Rosa lutea.

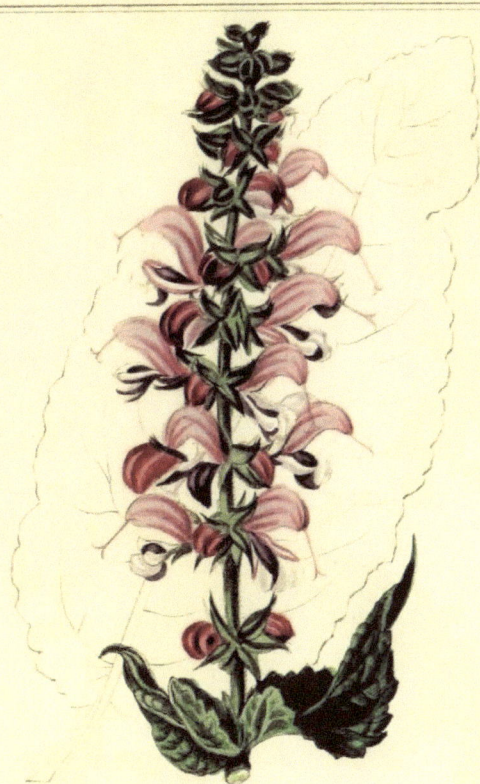
Salvia rugosa.

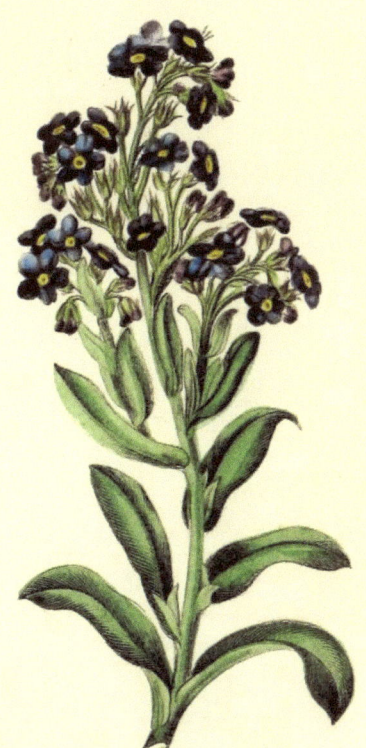
Myosotis Azoricus.

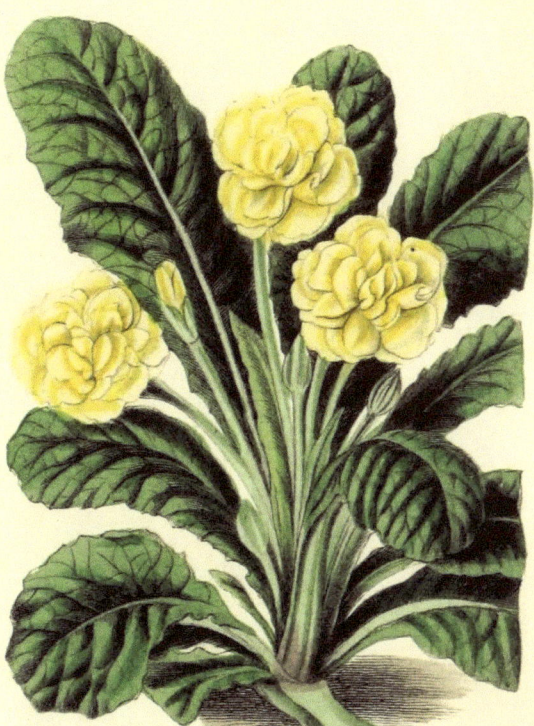
Primula acaulis.

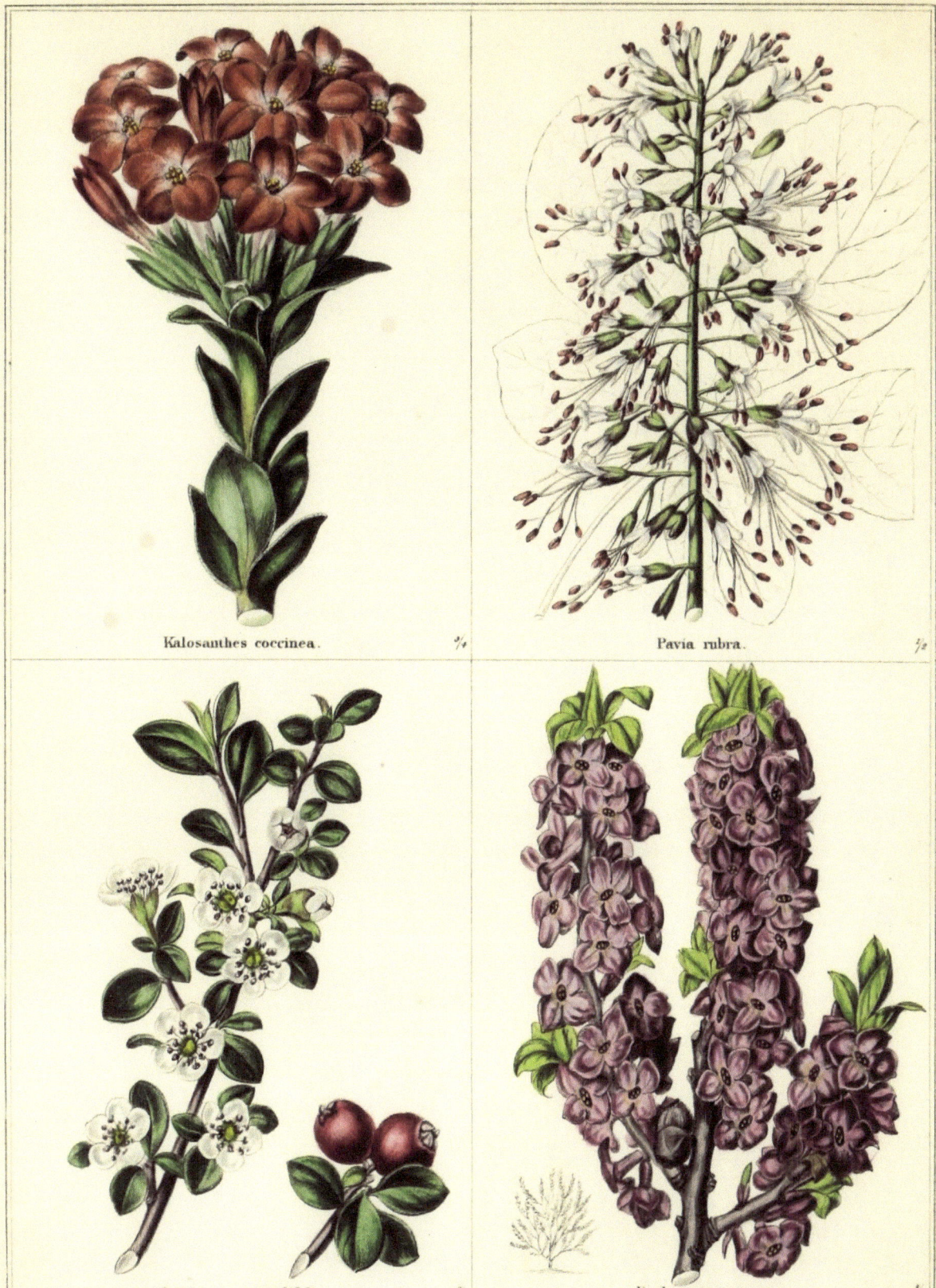

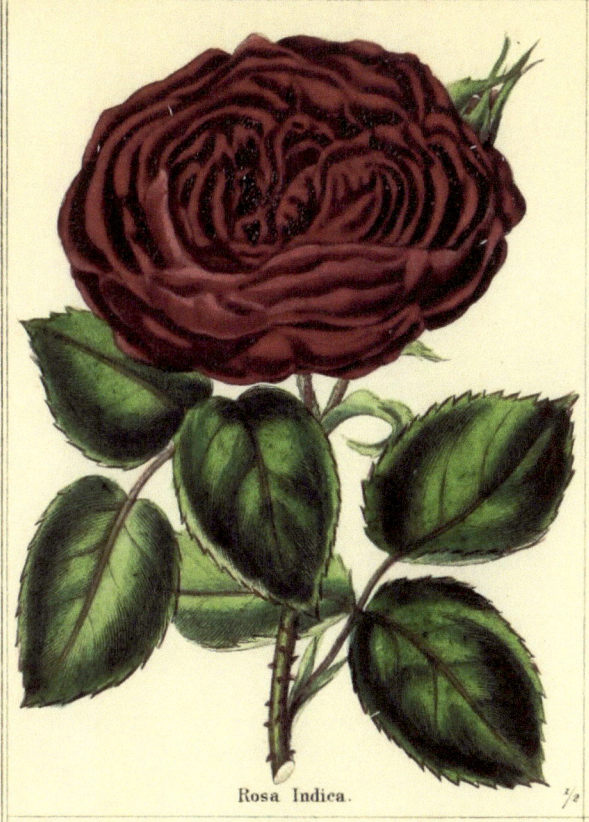

Rosa Indica.

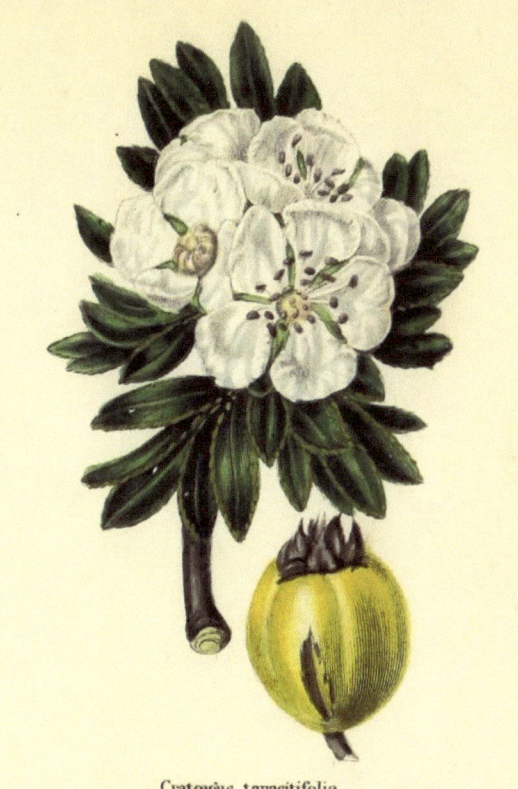

Cratœgus tanacitifolia.

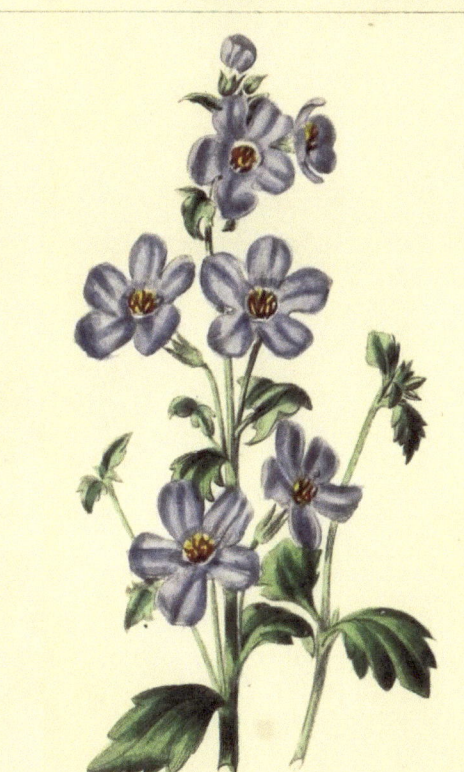

Chœnostoma polyanthum.

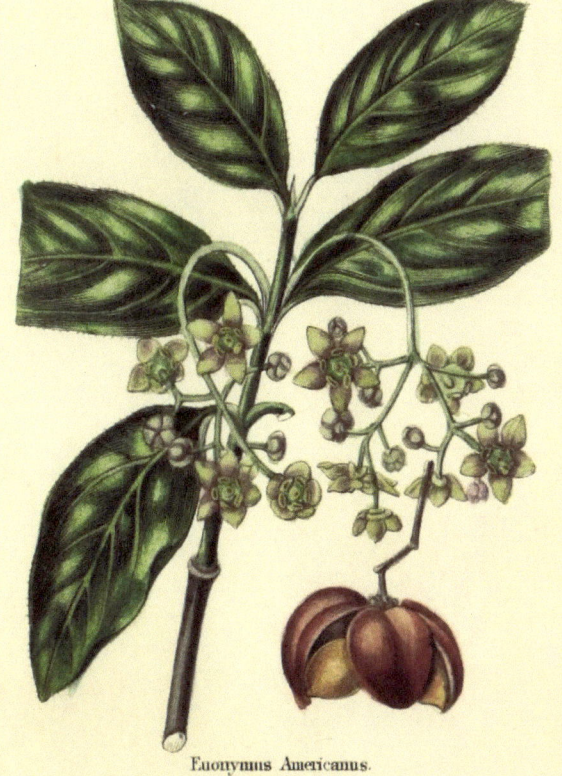

Euonymus Americanus.

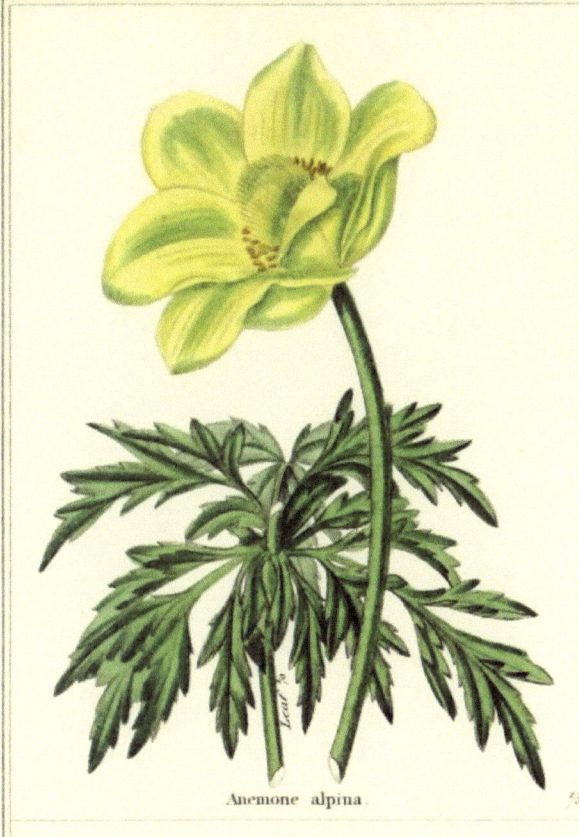
Anemone alpina.

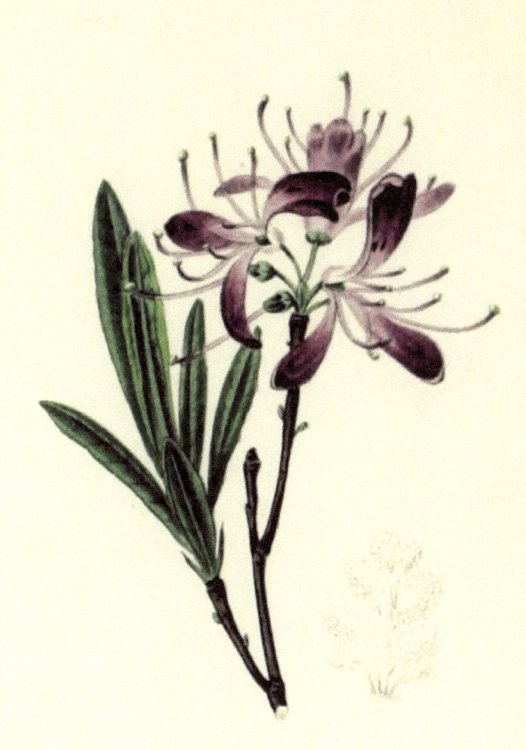
Rhodora Canadense.

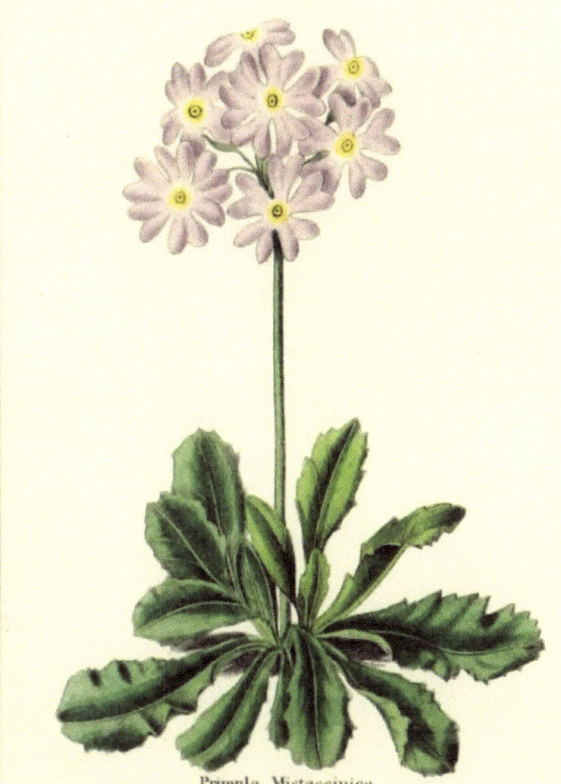
Primula Mistassinica.

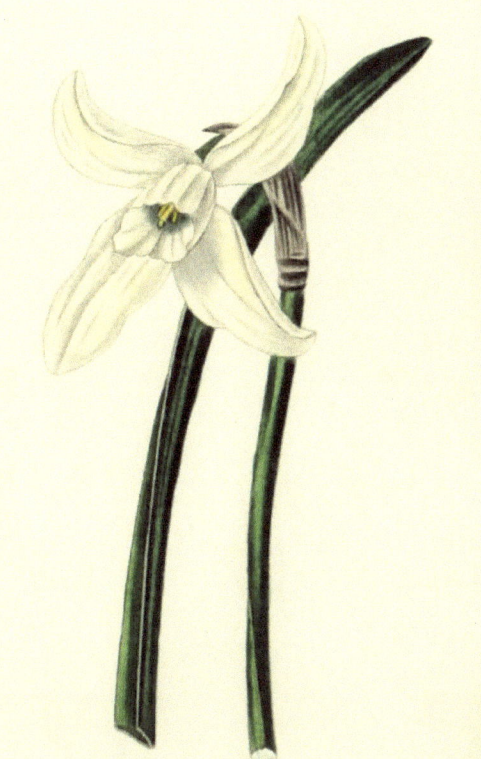
Narcissus montanus.

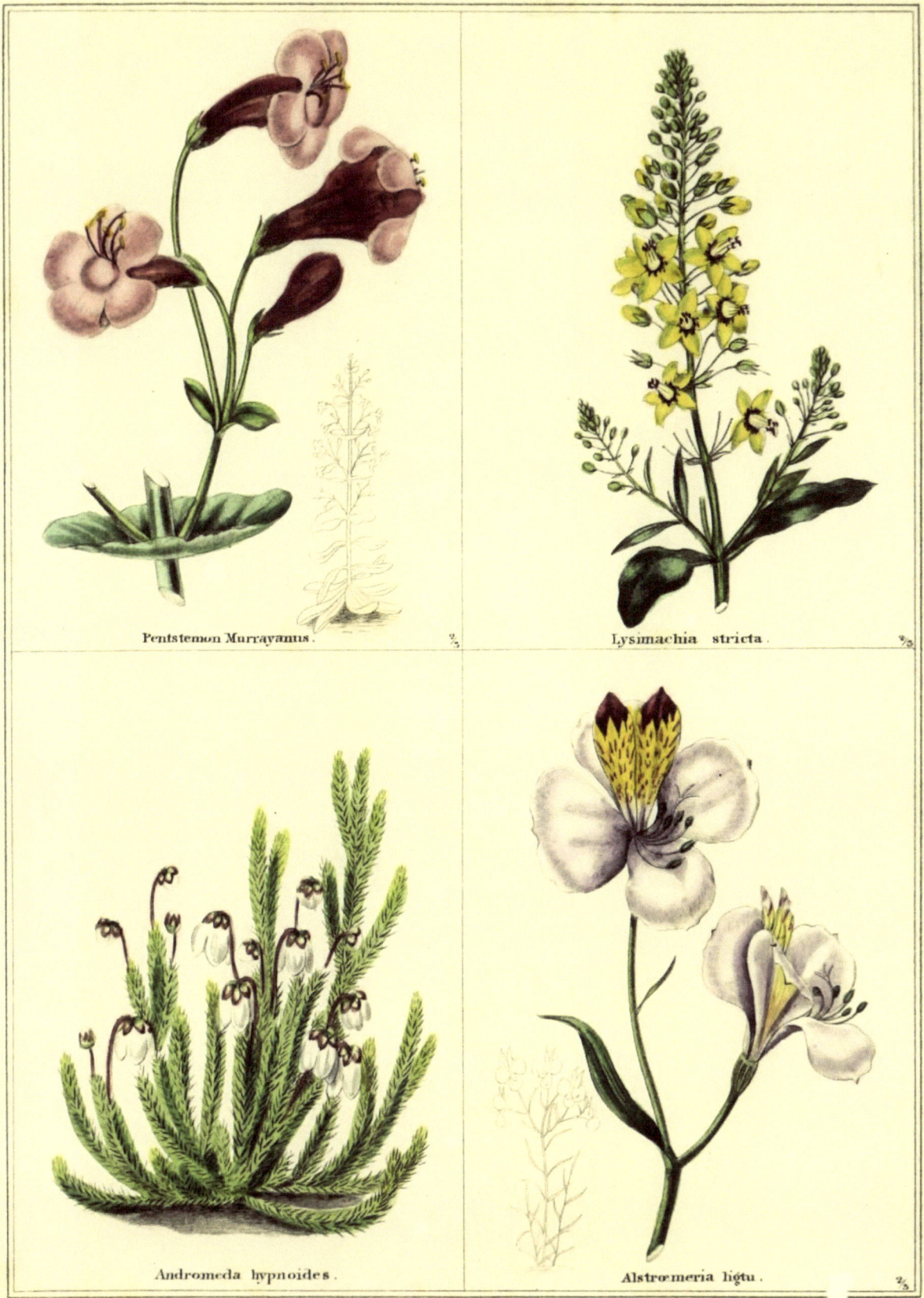

Pentstemon Murrayanus.　　Lysimachia stricta.

Andromeda hypnoides.　　Alstromeria ligtu.

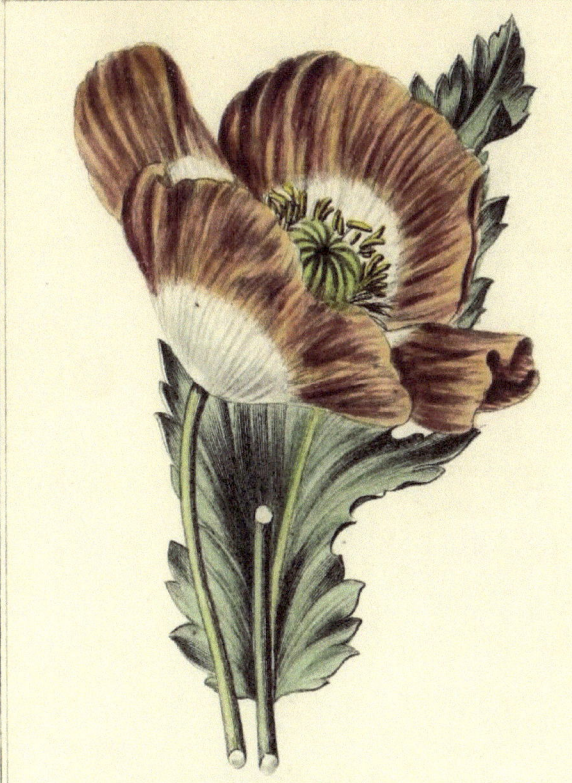
Papaver amœnum.

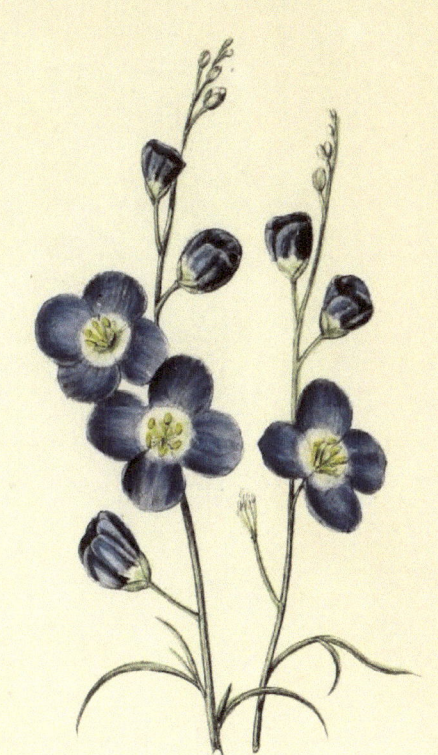
Heliophila trifida.

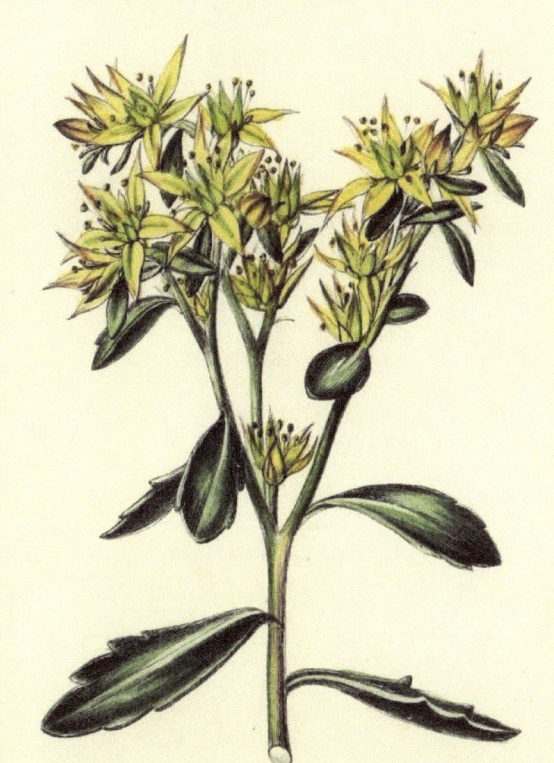
Sedum Kamtschatkia.

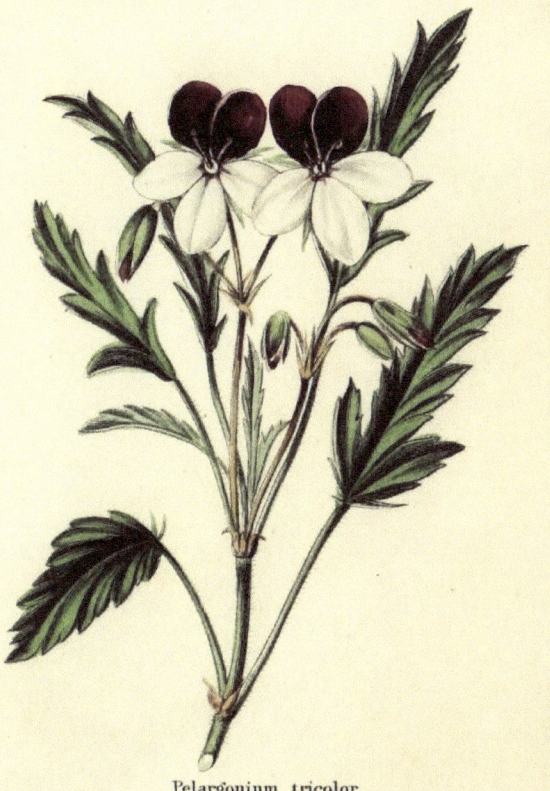
Pelargonium tricolor.

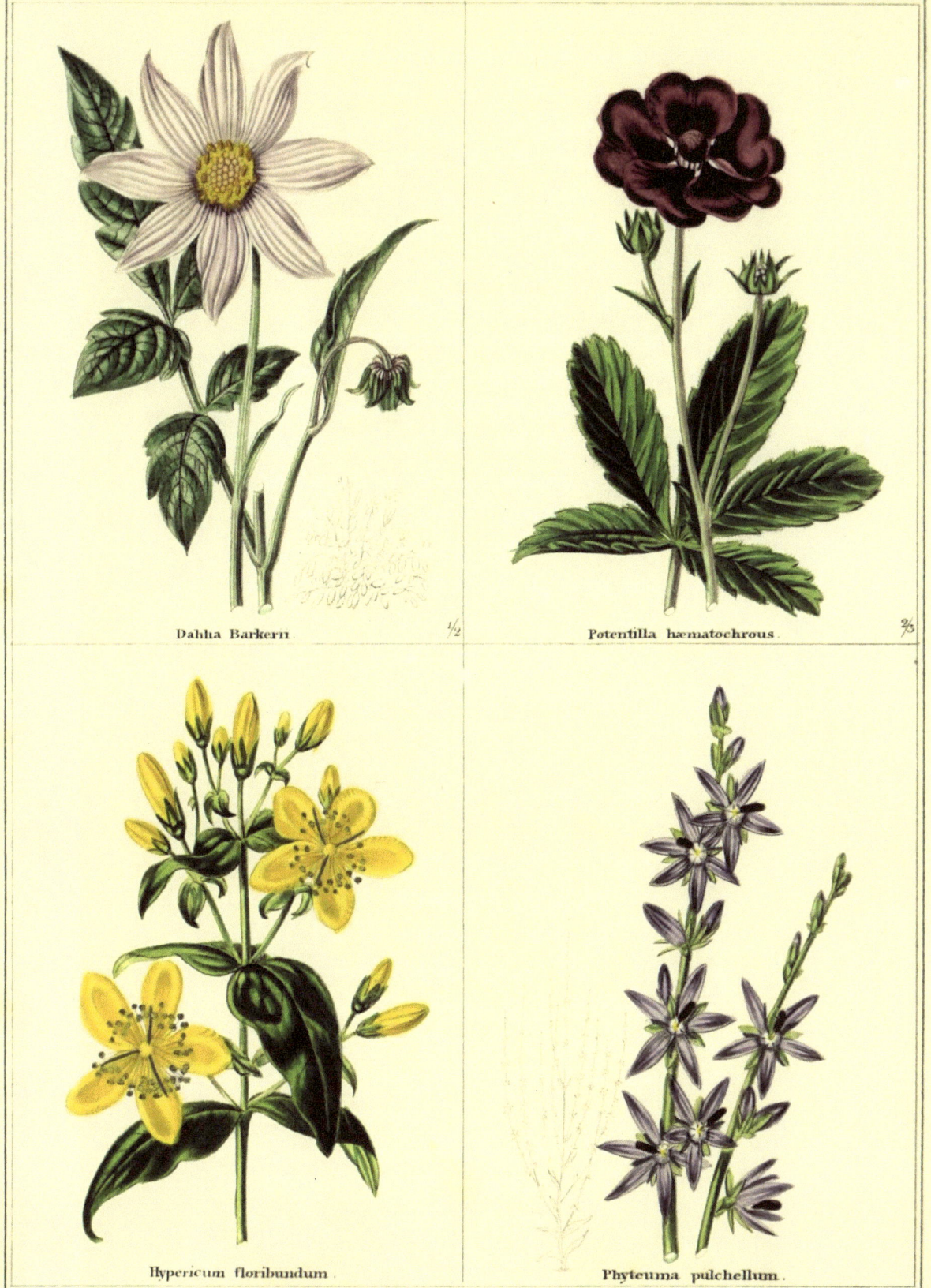

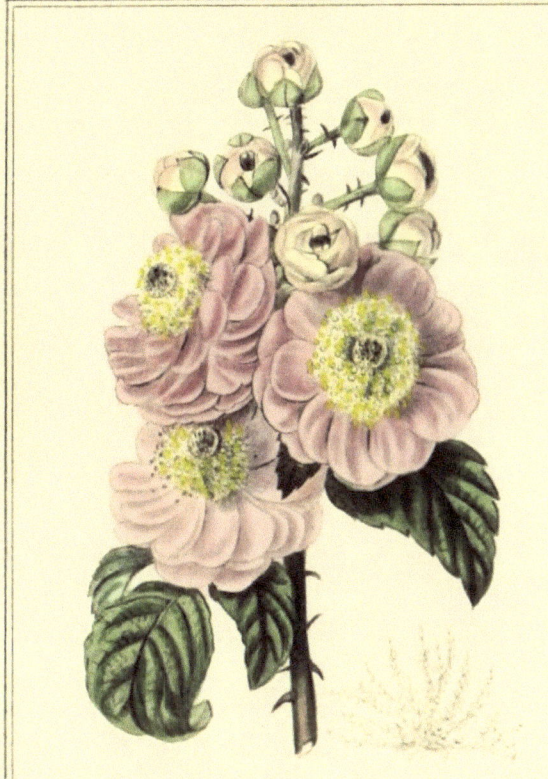
Rubus fruticosus.

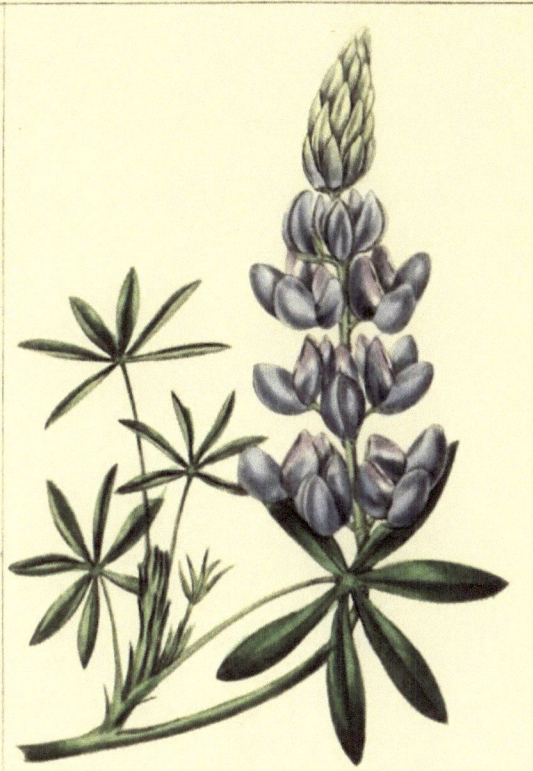
Lupinus nanus.

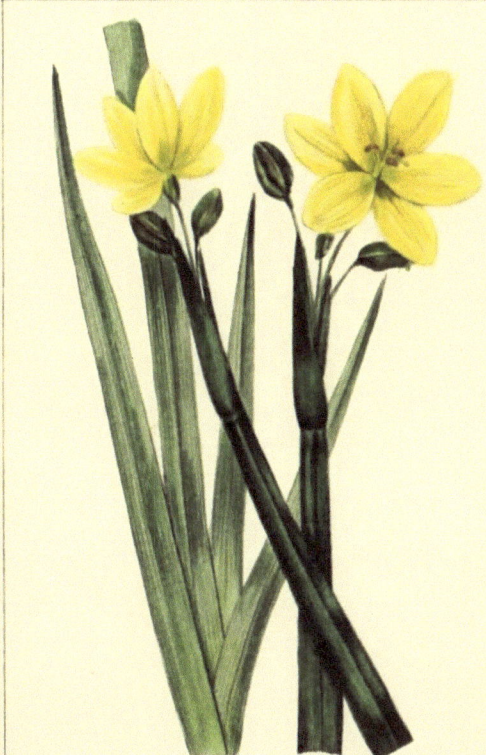
Sisyrinchium californicum.

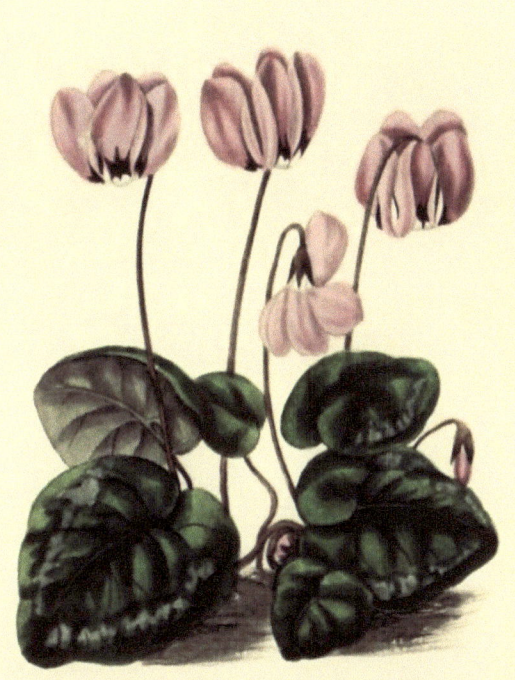
Cyclamen vernum.

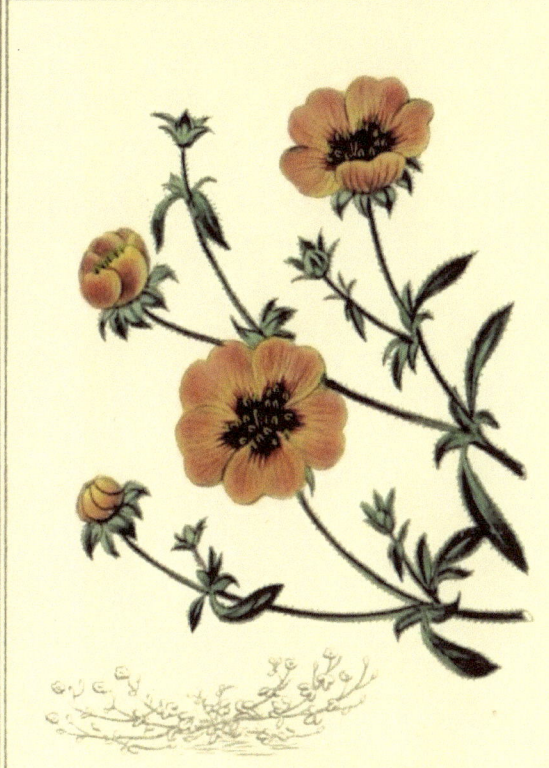
Potentilla tormentillo-formosa.

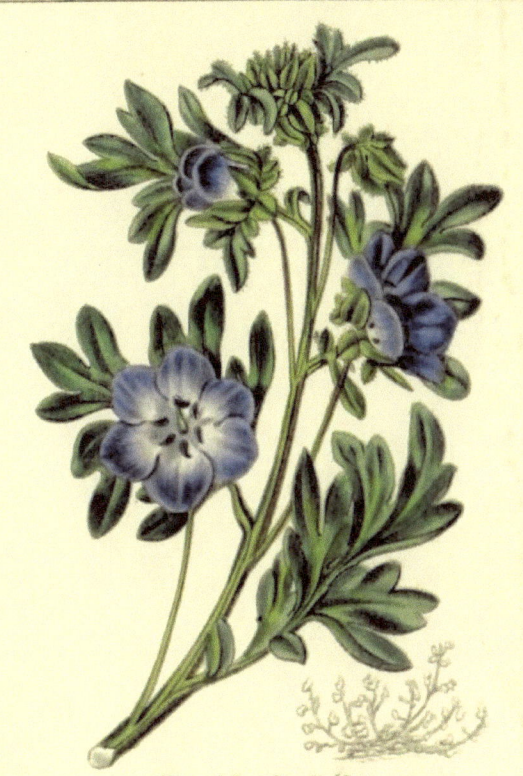
Nemophila phacelioides.

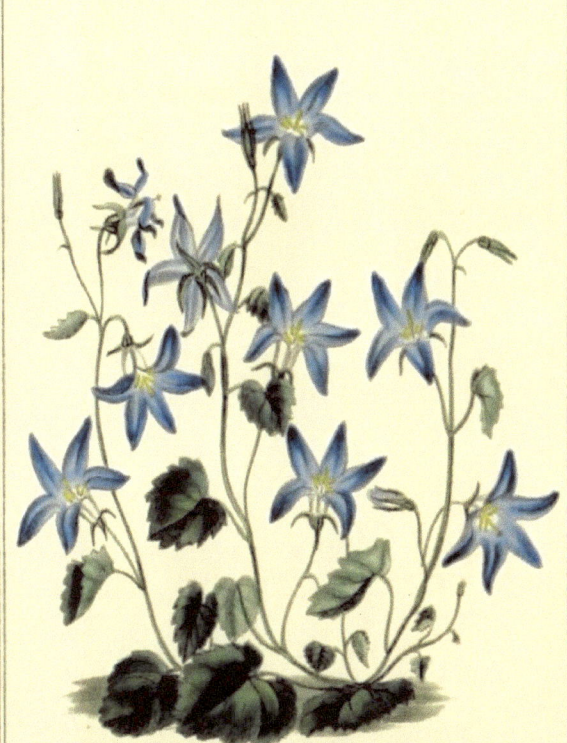
Campanula garganica.

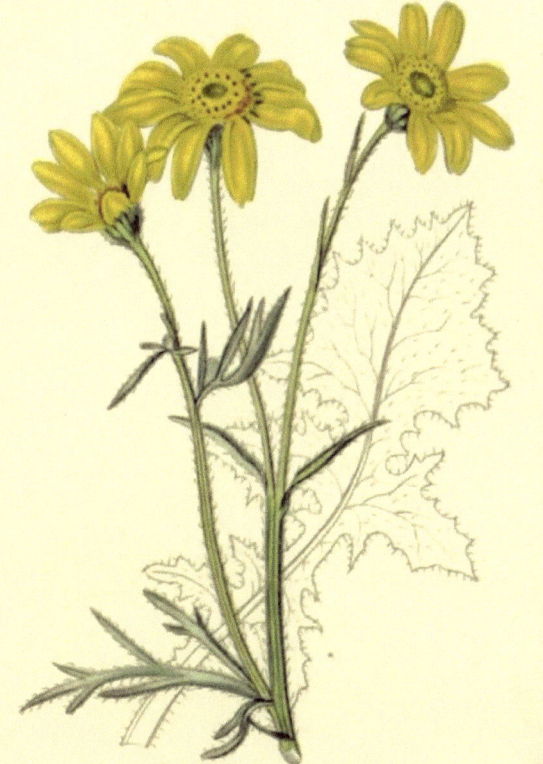
Eriophyllum cæspitosum.

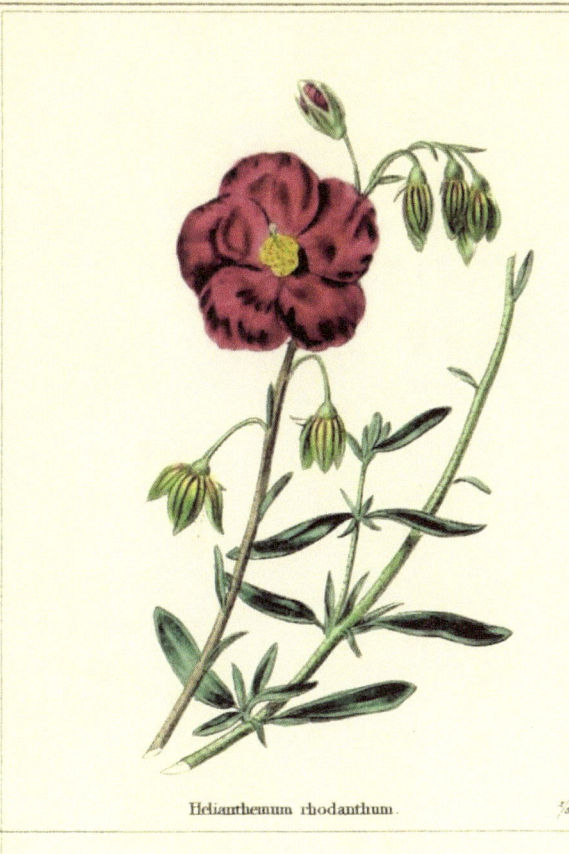
Helianthemum rhodanthum.

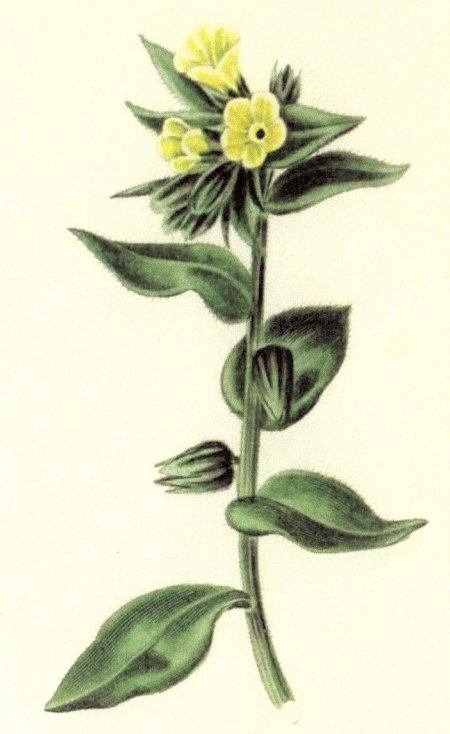
Nonea flavescens.

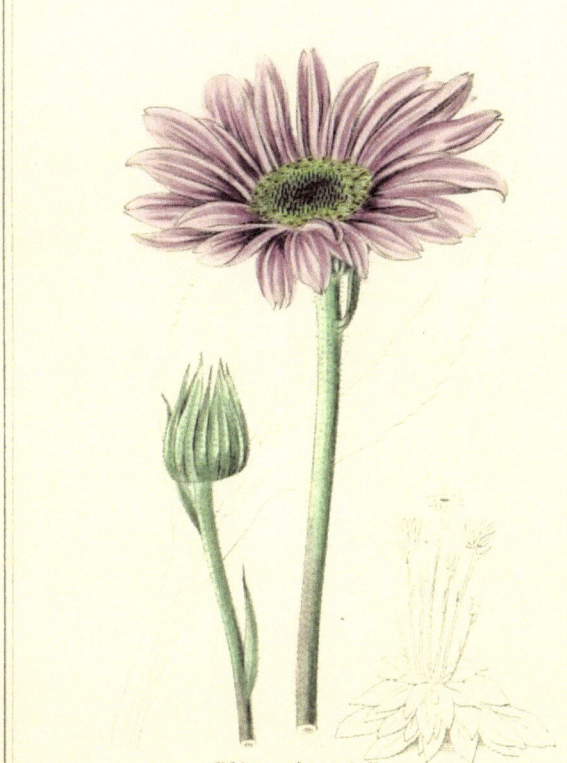
Echinacea heterophylla.

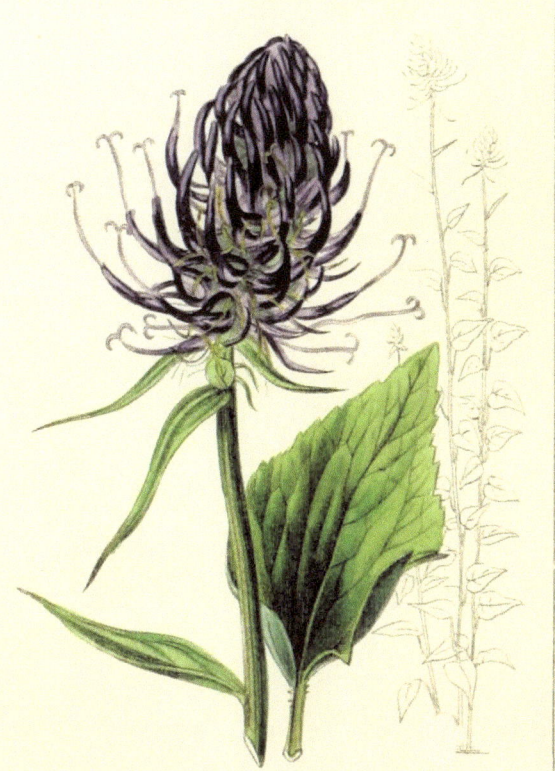
Phyteuma Halleri.

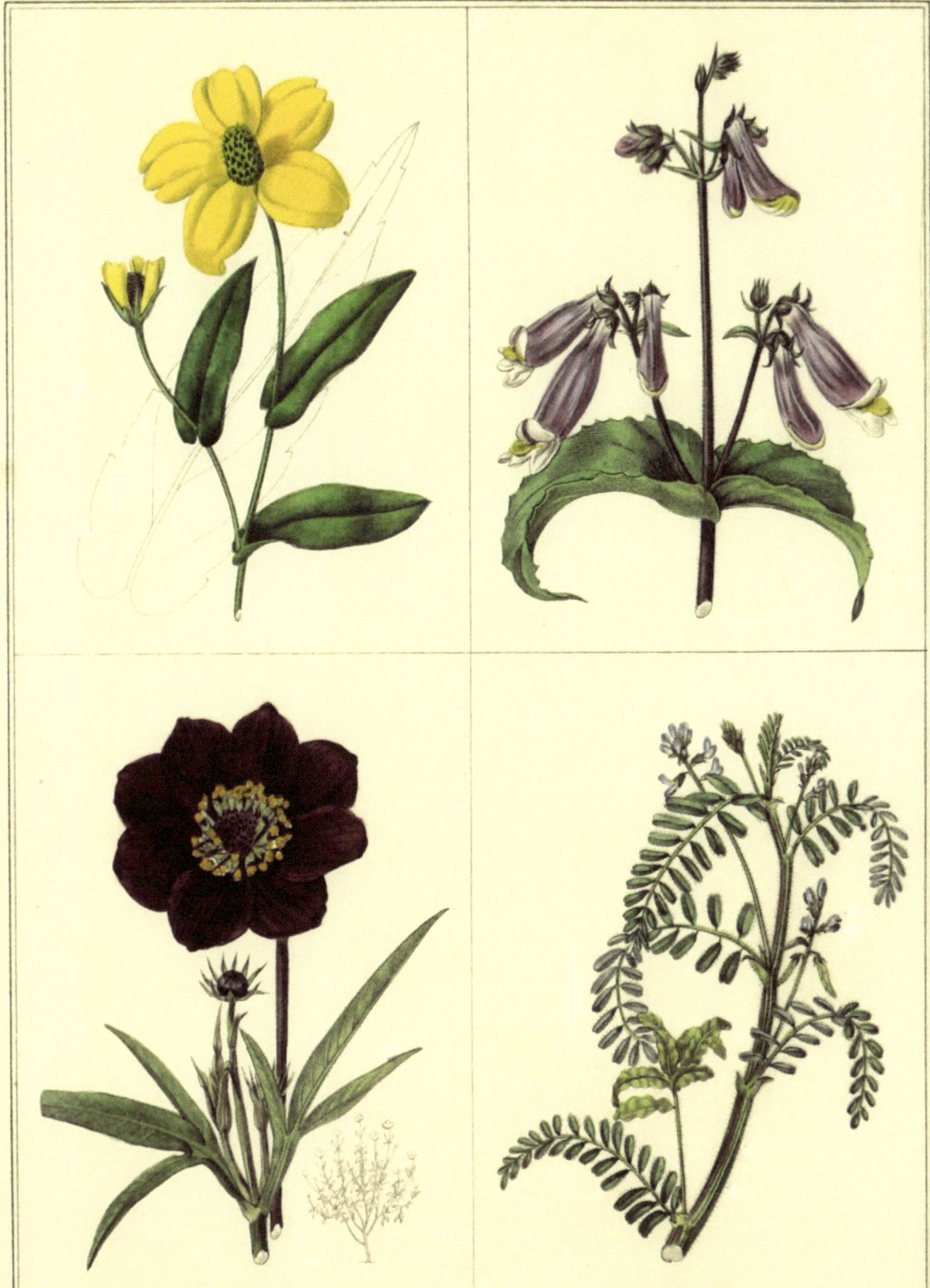

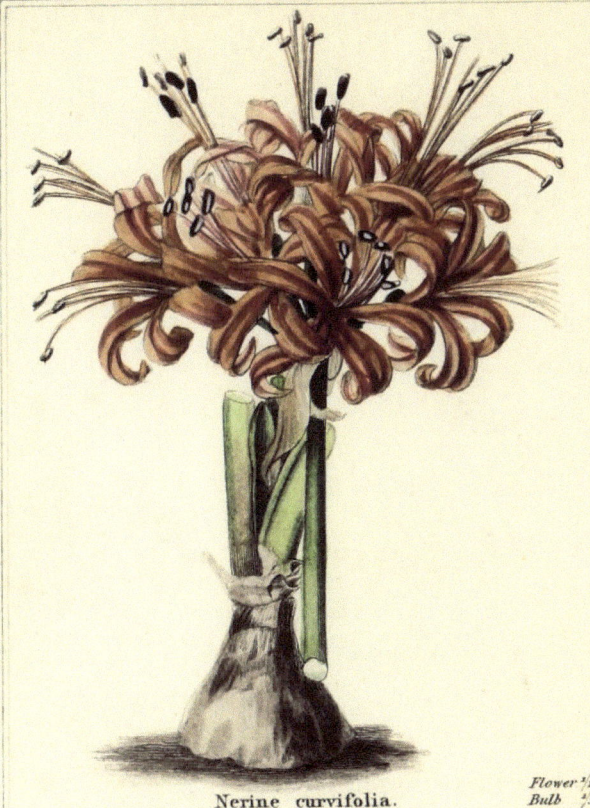

Nerine curvifolia. Flower ½ Bulb ⅔

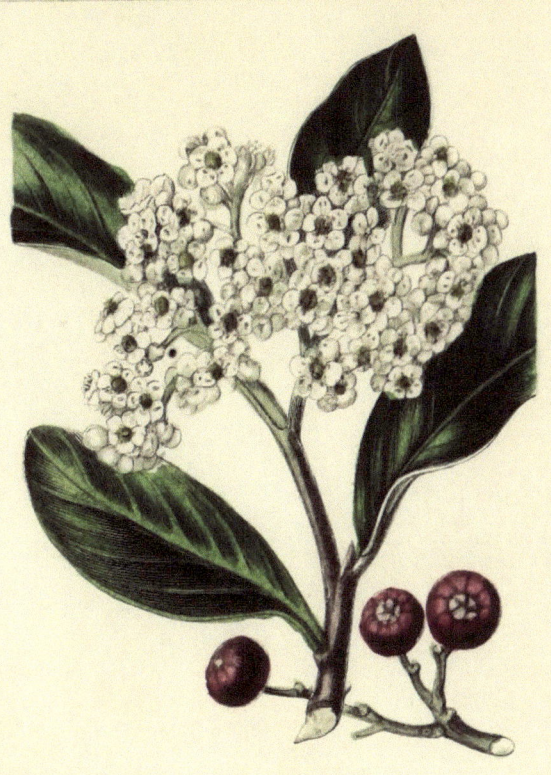

Cotoneaster frigida. ⅔

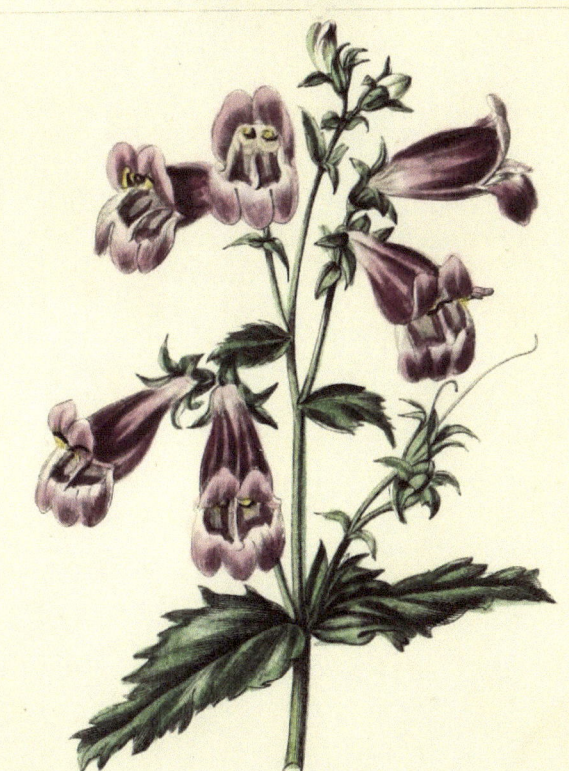

Pentstemon diffusum. ¾

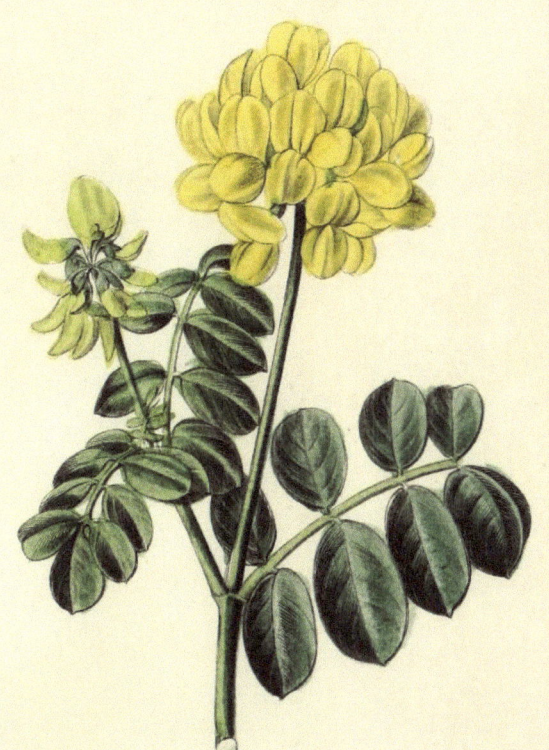

Coronilla glauca. ¾

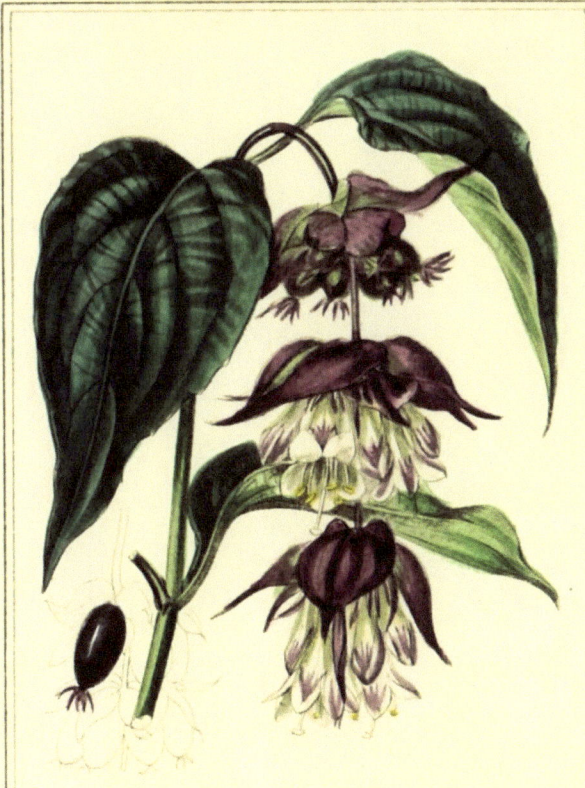

Leycesteria formosa

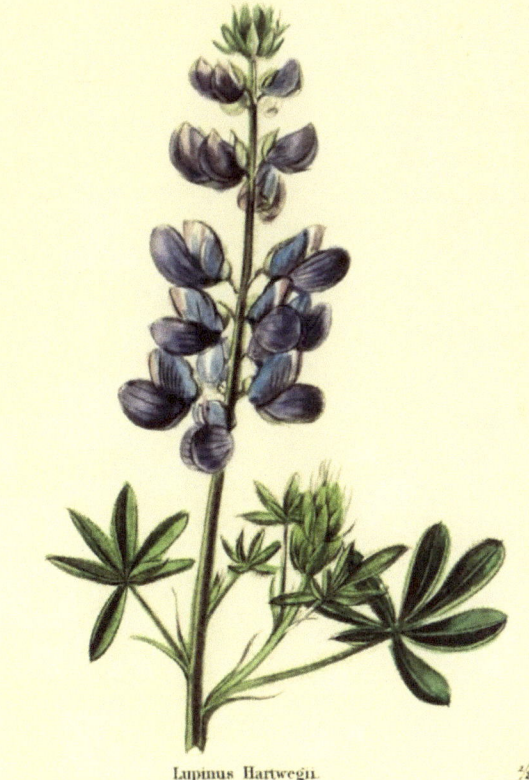

Lupinus Hartwegii

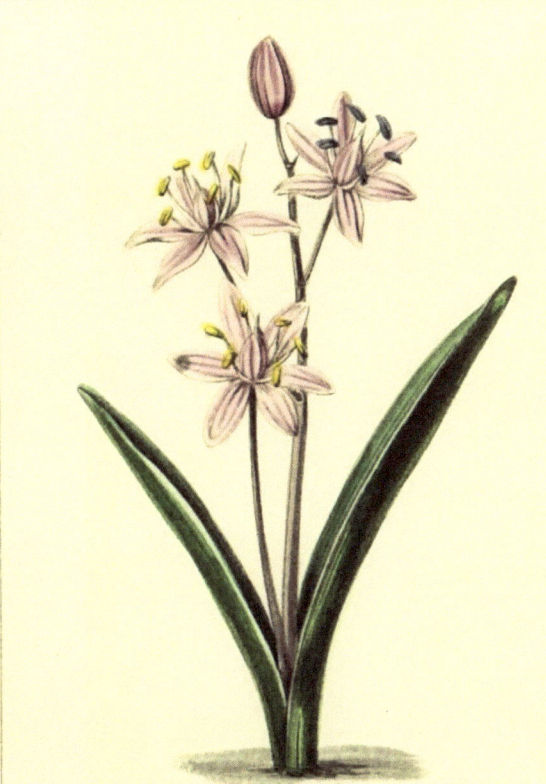

Scilla bifolia rubra

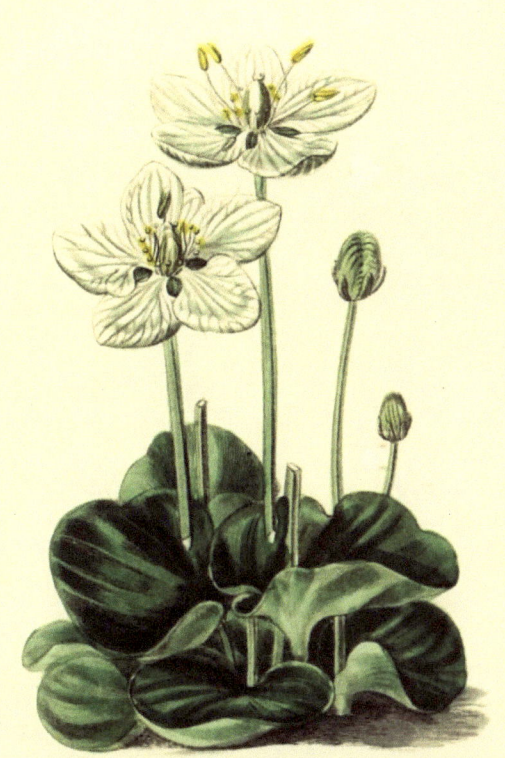

Parnassia asarifolia

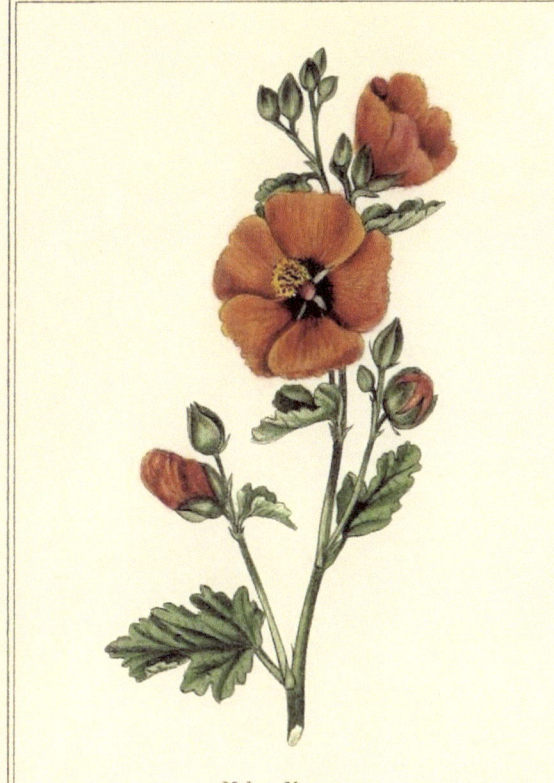
Malva Munroana.

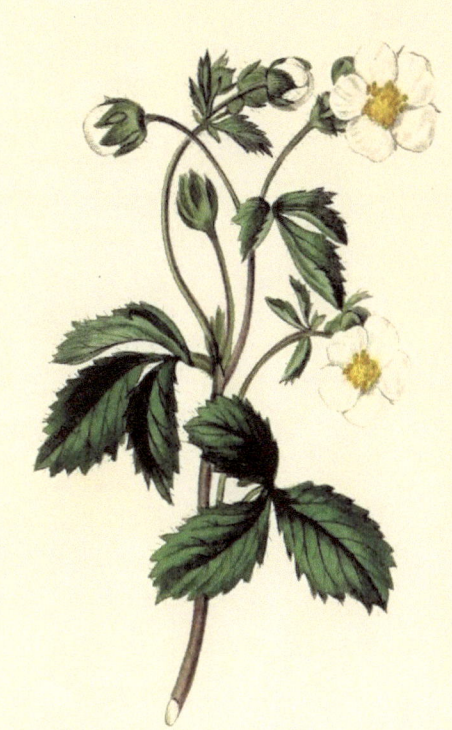
Potentilla rupestris.

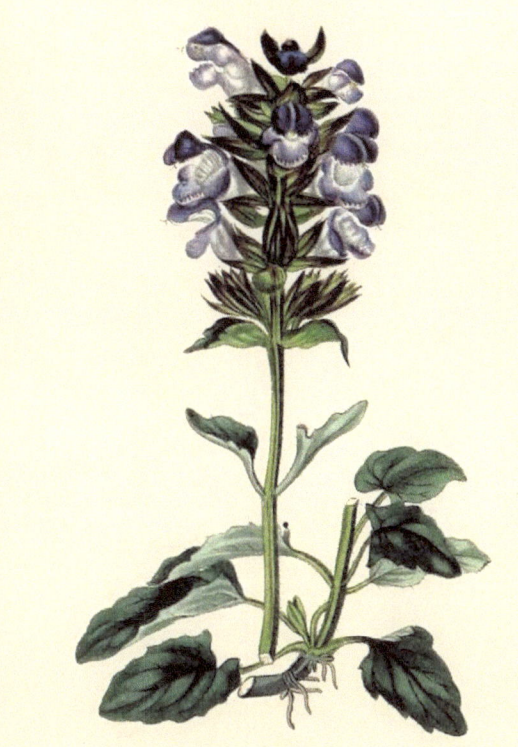
Prunella Sibirica.

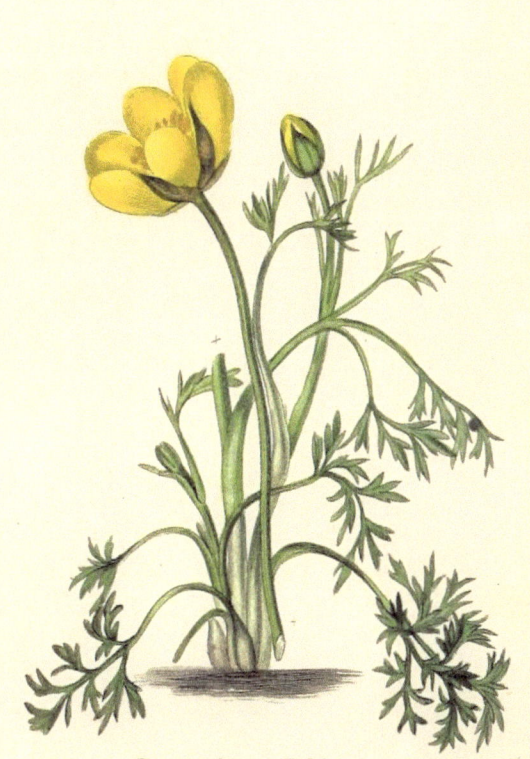
Ranunculus millefoliatus.

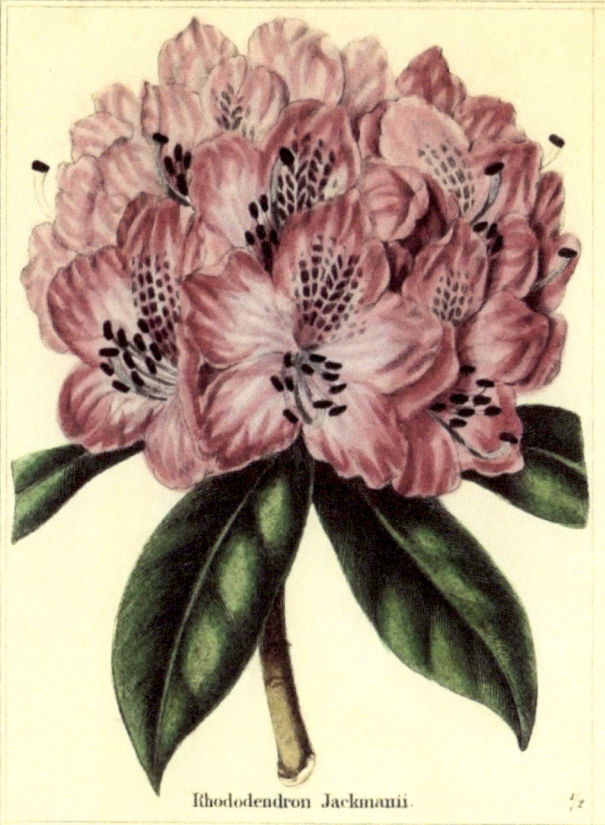

Rhododendron Jackmanii. 1/2

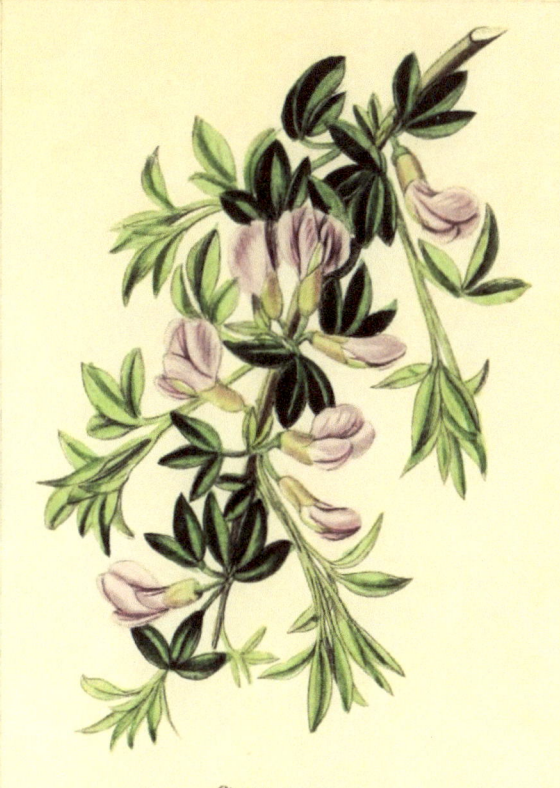

Cistus purpureus. 2/3

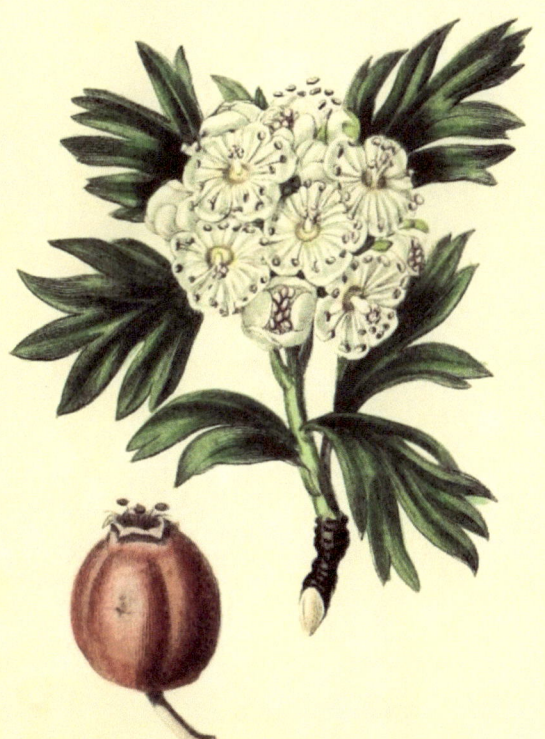

Cratægus odoratissima. 2/3

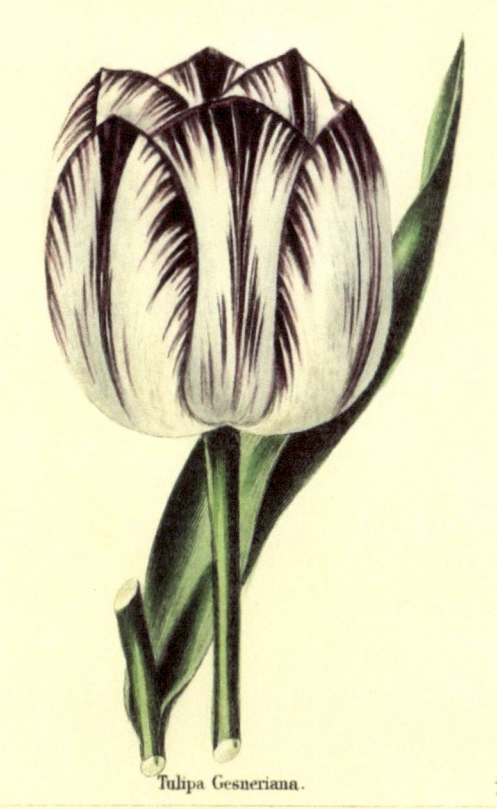

Tulipa Gesneriana. 1/2

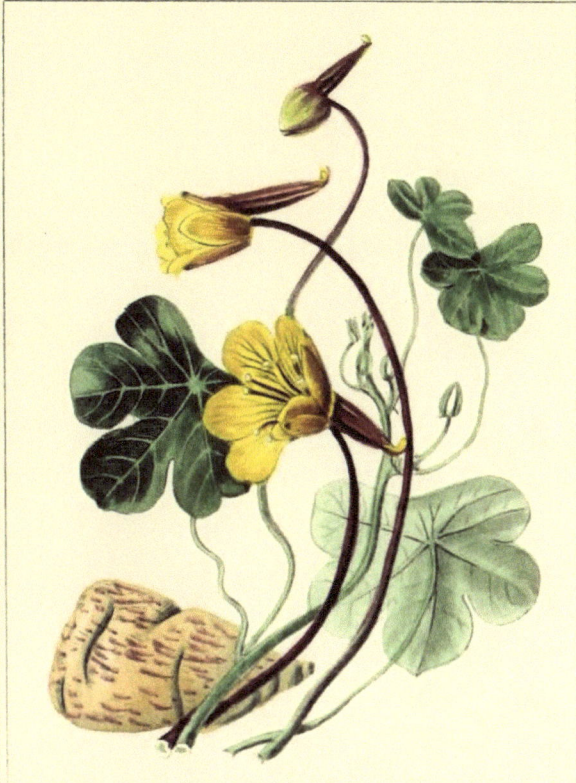
Tropæolum tuberosum.

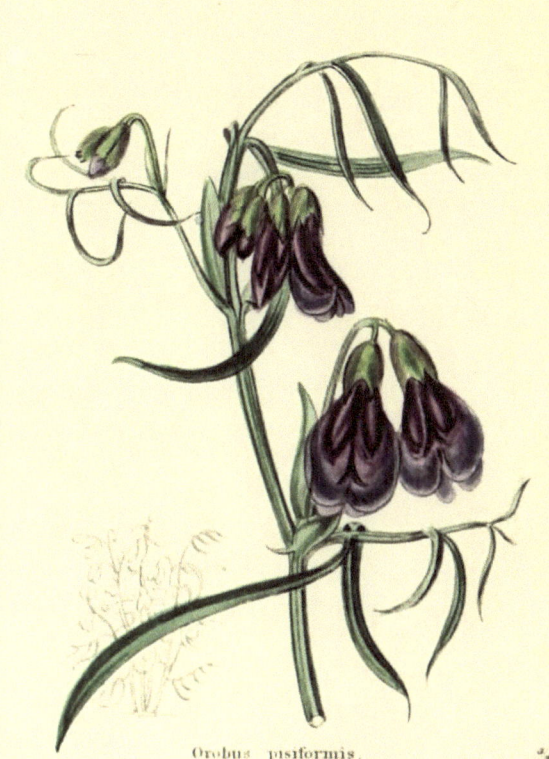
Orobus pisiformis.

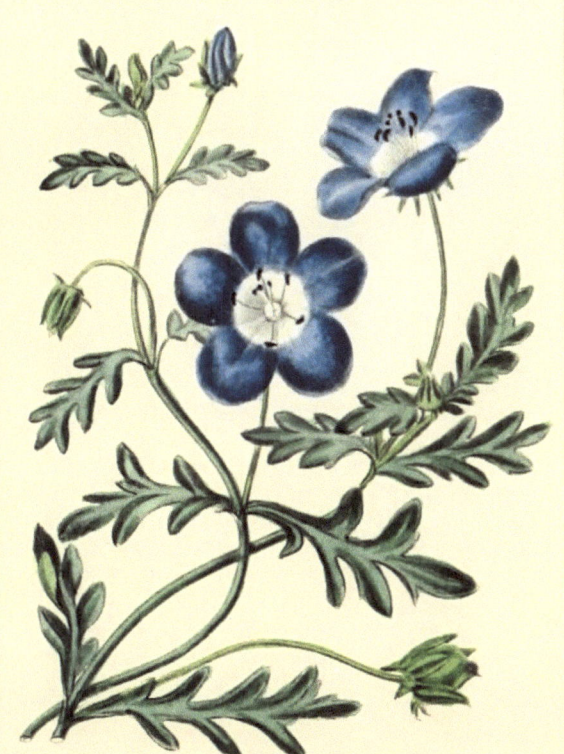
Nemophila insignis.

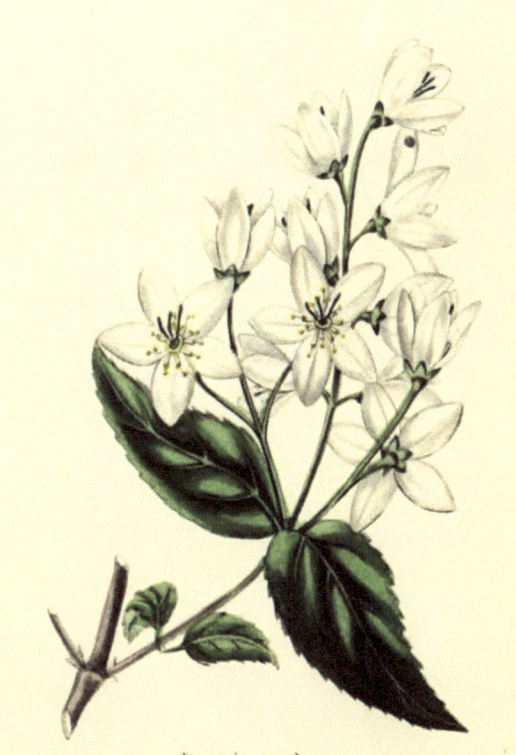
Deutzia scabra.

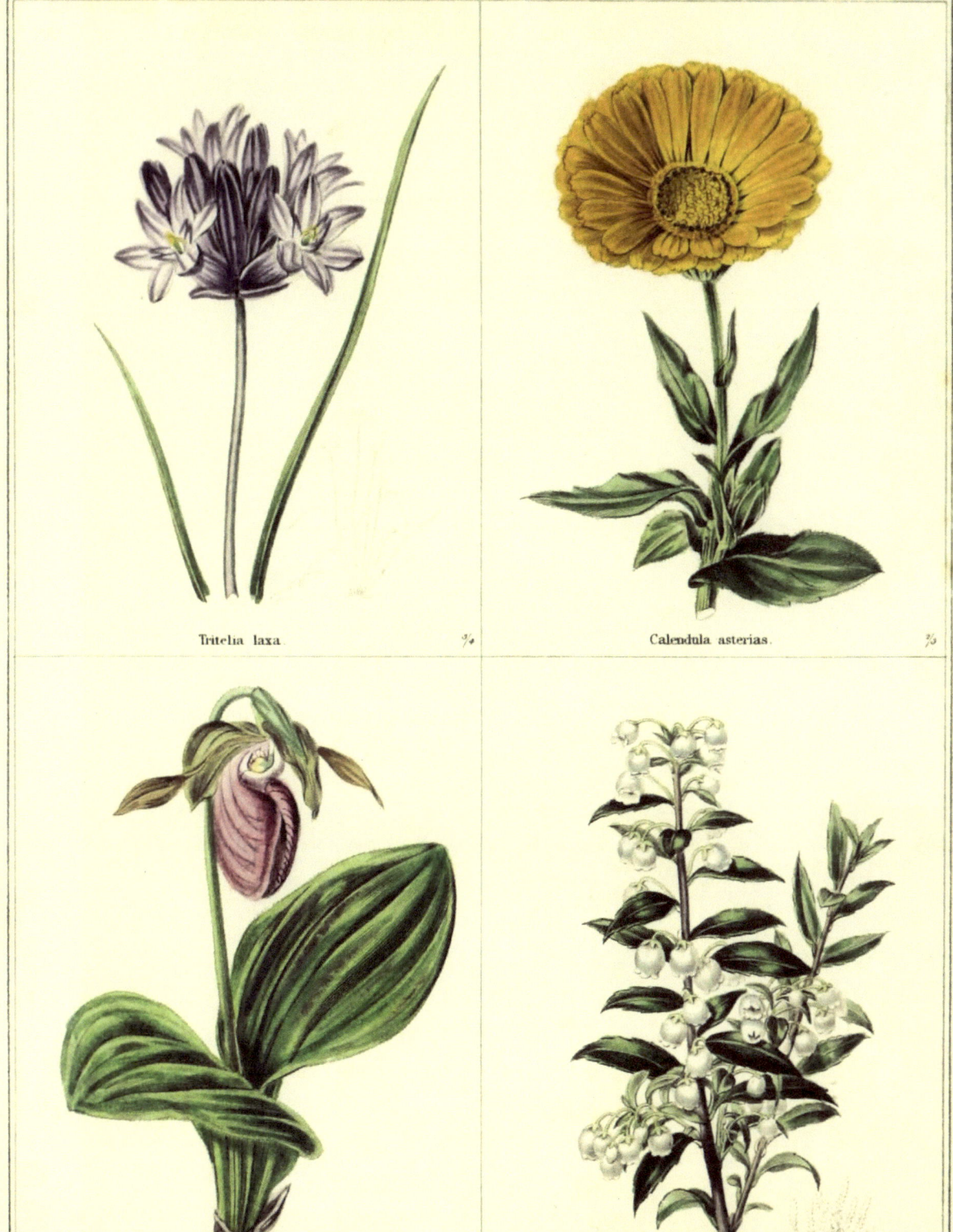

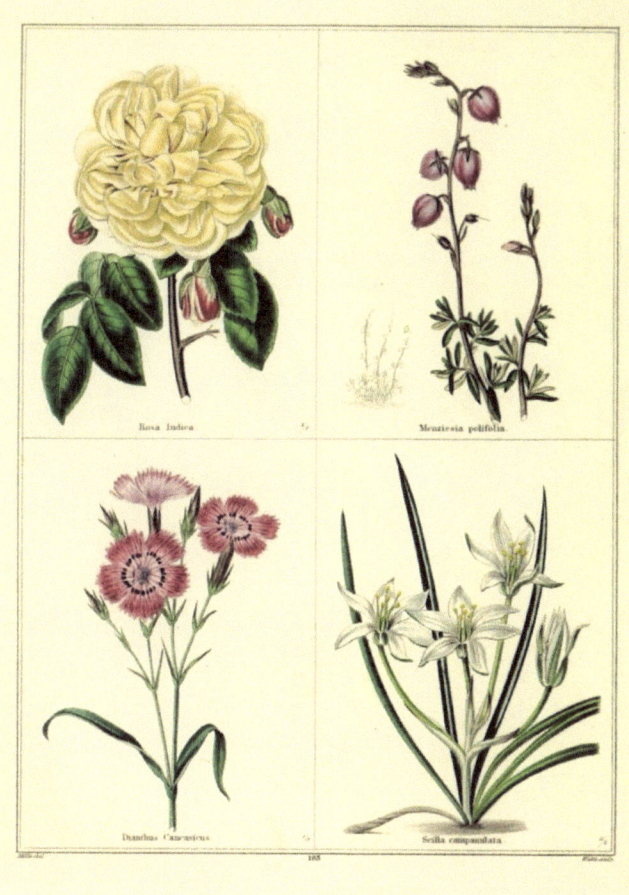
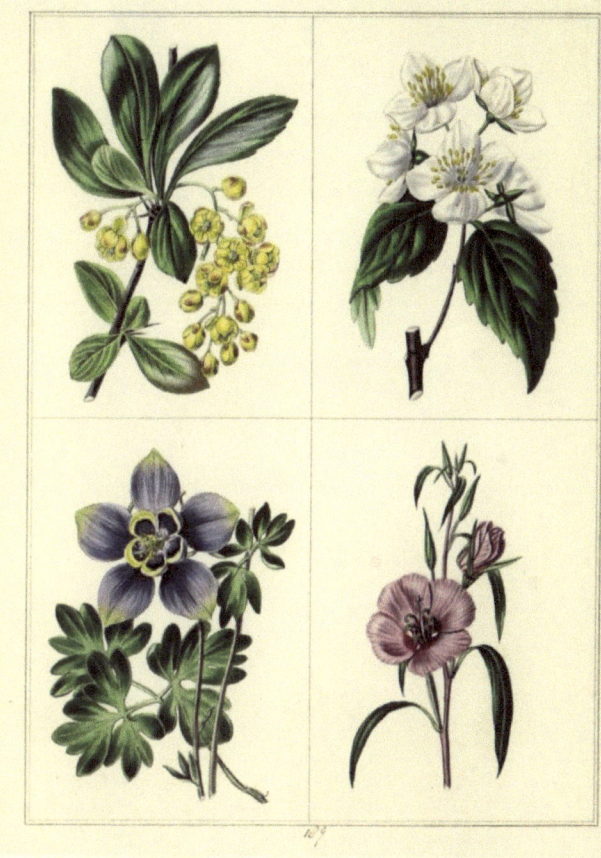
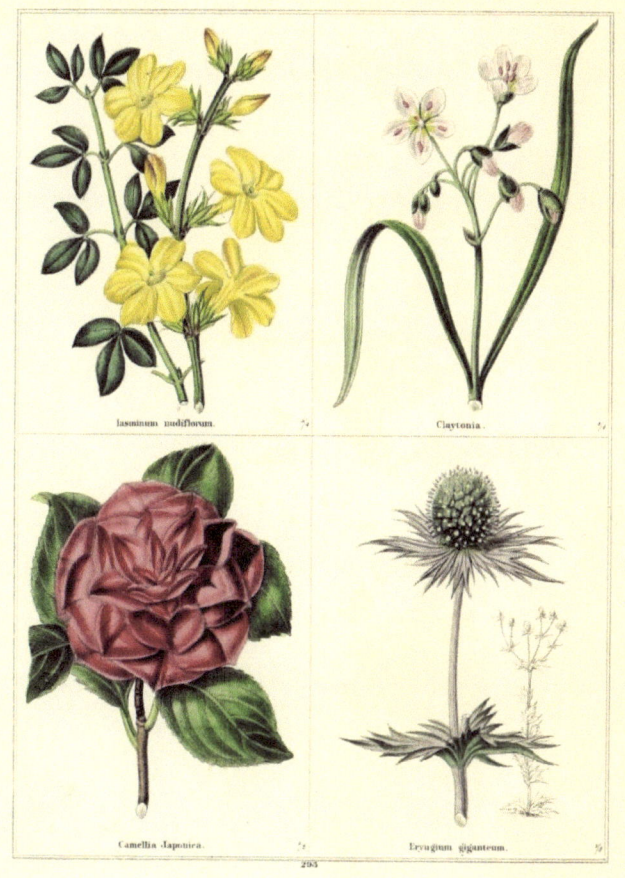
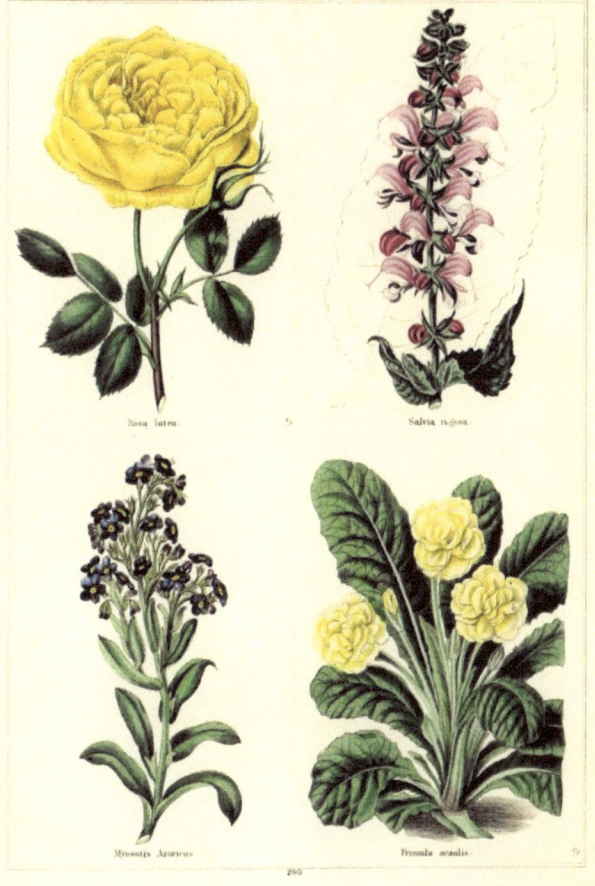

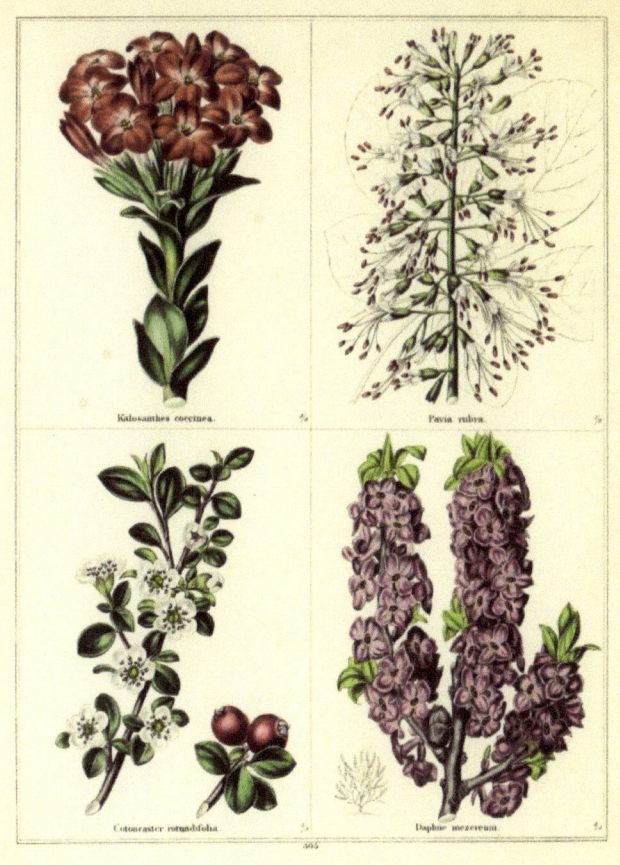
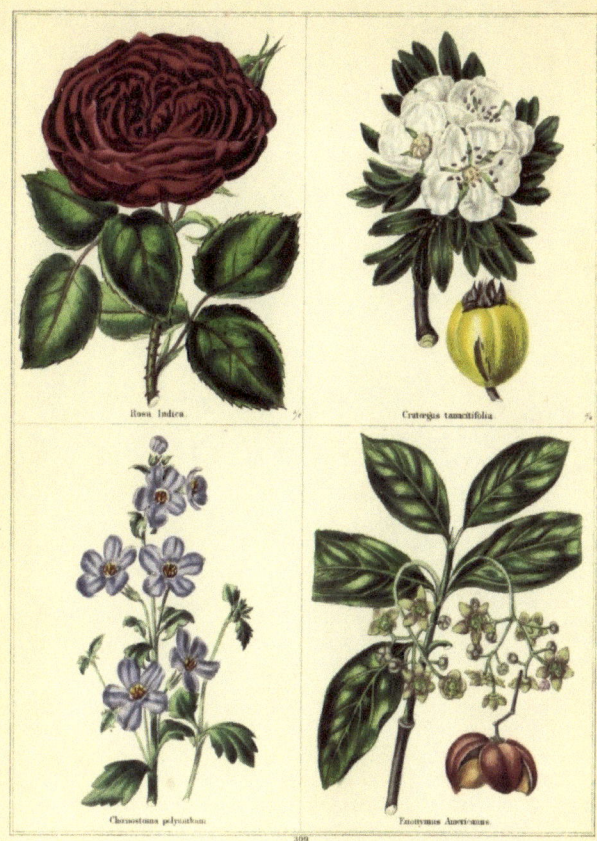
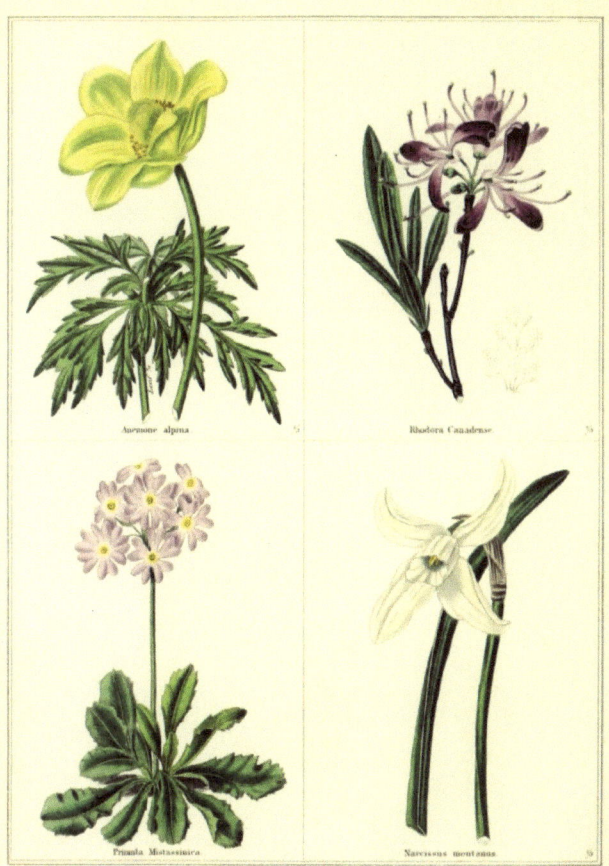
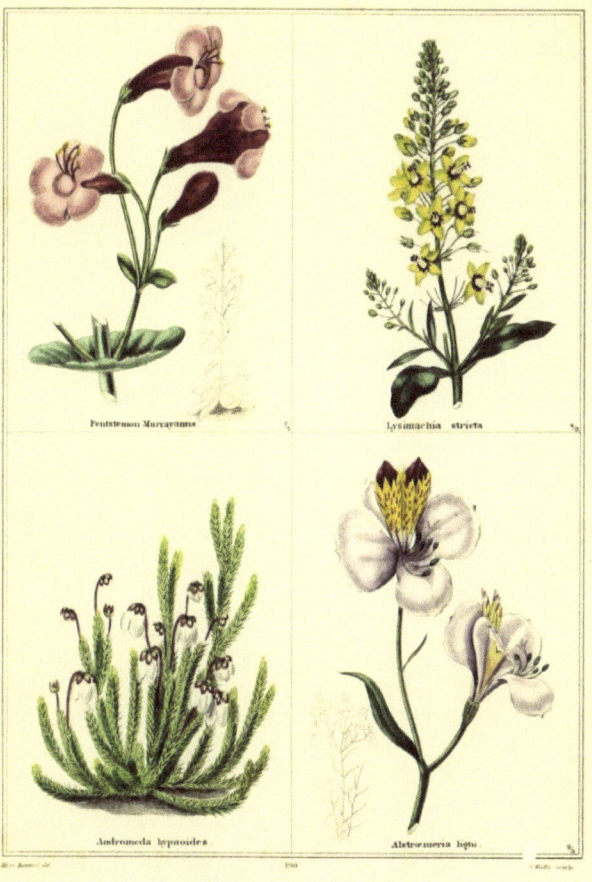

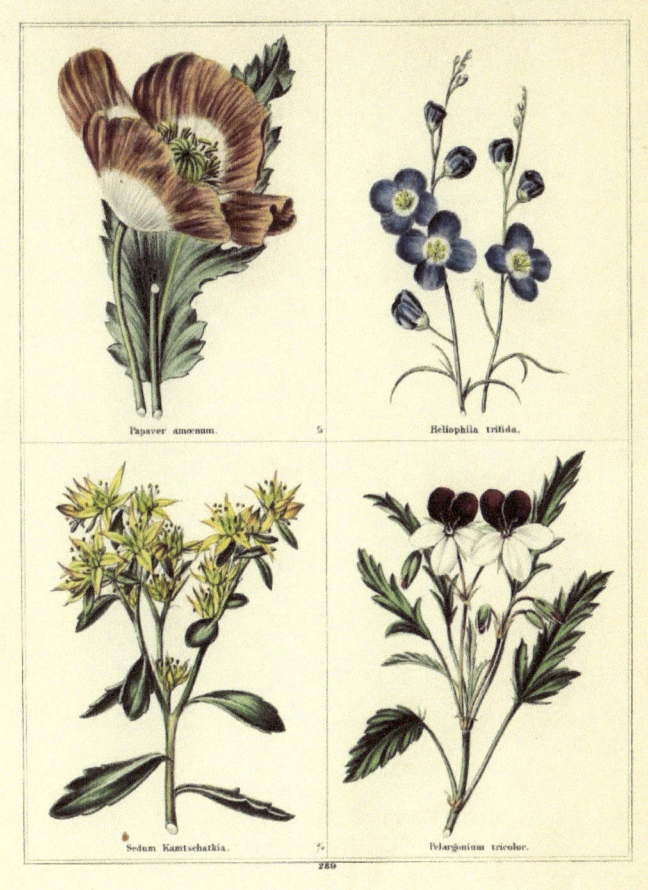
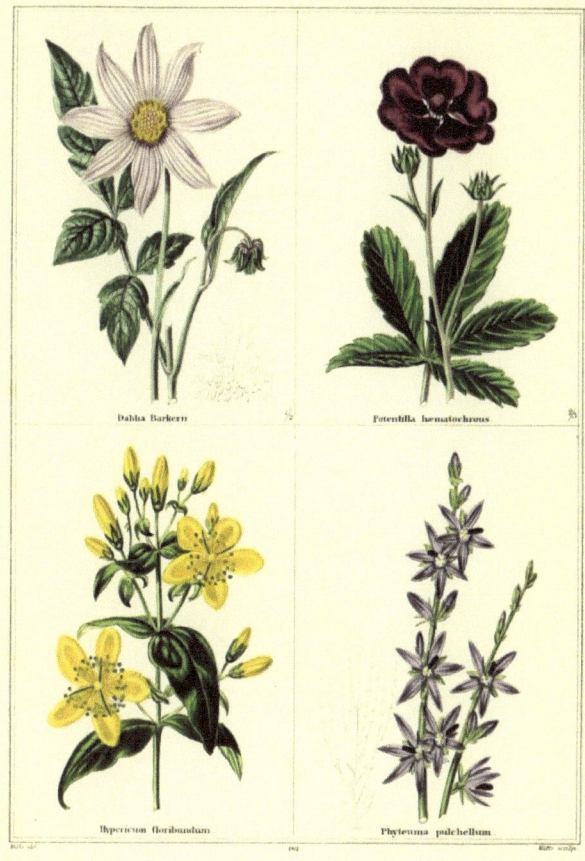
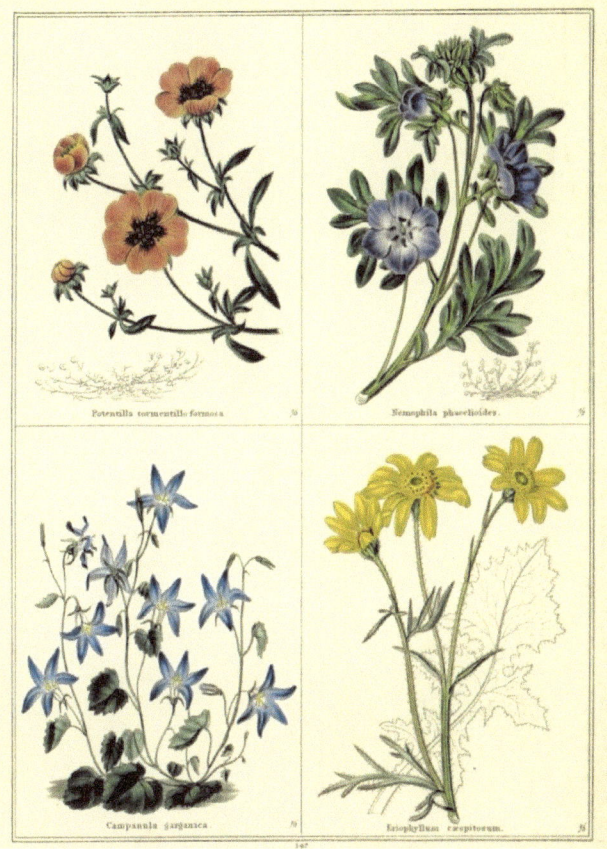
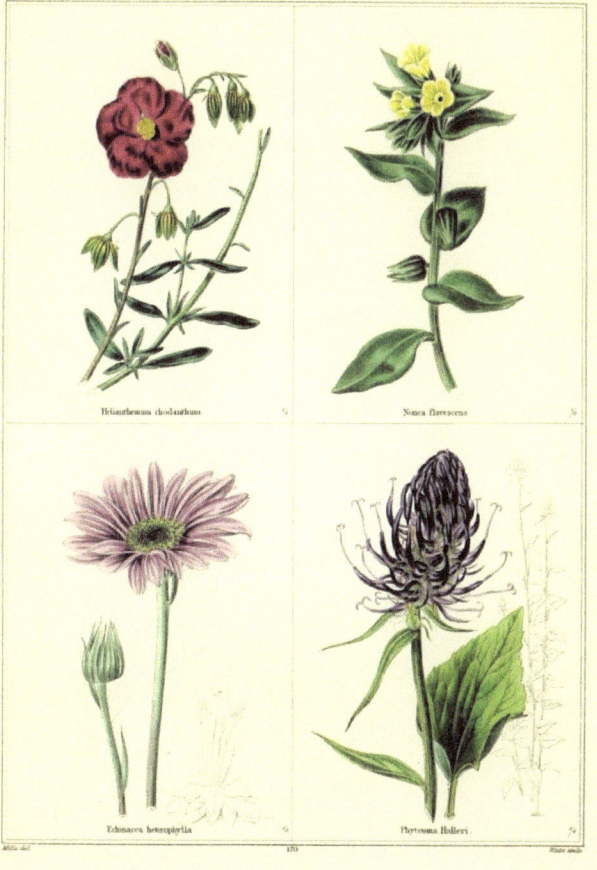

www.ingramcontent.com/pod-product-compliance
Lightning Source LLC
Chambersburg PA
CBHW042322250526
R18347200002B/R183472PG45473CBX00008B/7